OUT ON A LIMB

An autobiography by
GERARD BOURKE

Thailand 2003

Printed in Victoria, Canada

Note for Librarians: a cataloguing record for this book that includes Dewey Classification and US Library of Congress numbers is available from the National Library of Canada. The complete cataloguing record can be obtained from the National Library's online database at:
www.nlc-bnc.ca/amicus/index-e.html
ISBN 1-4120-0969-3

TRAFFORD

This book was published *on-demand* in cooperation with Trafford Publishing.
On-demand publishing is a unique process and service of making a book available for retail sale to the public taking advantage of on-demand manufacturing and Internet marketing.
On-demand publishing includes promotions, retail sales, manufacturing, order fulfilment, accounting and collecting royalties on behalf of the author.

Suite 6E, 2333 Government St., Victoria, B.C. V8T 4P4, CANADA
Phone	250-383-6864	Toll-free	1-888-232-4444 (Canada & US)
Fax	250-383-6804	E-mail	sales@trafford.com
Web site	www.trafford.com	TRAFFORD PUBLISHING IS A DIVISION OF TRAFFORD HOLDINGS LTD.
Trafford Catalogue #03-1338	www.trafford.com/robots/03-1338.html	

10   9   8   7   6   5   4

For Nancy, Dan, Sirilac and Na.

OUT ON A LIMB
Or
"The King of love my shepherd is"

By

GERARD BOURKE

Chapters:

Chapter one

The Vital Years 1811 to 1911

It is a sobering thought how nearly I never existed. What if the soldier who shot my great-great-grandfather through the jaw at the battle of the Helde in Holland in 1801, when he was a young ensign in the Grenadier Guards had aimed an inch higher? Yet it evidently did not impede him too badly, since a year later he married his namesake Elizabeth Jane Bourke, daughter of the collector of taxes for Middlesex, John Bourke, who was a friend of the statesman Edmund Burke, to whom my family is related. He had already taken a law degree at Oxford, and often spent holidays at Burke's home at Beaconsfield when at Westminster school.

General Sir Richard, 1777-1855, later became the eighth (1831-37) governor of New South Wales, as the early governors were then styled, it being two-thirds the land mass of Australia, after being lieutenant governor of the eastern provinces of the Cape from 1827-28. It was while superintendent of the military academy at High Wycombe near London in 1811, where in addition to military matters he taught Spanish, classics and law, that he bought Thornfields, or Shanavoy as it was then known, a small estate of about 180 acres, six miles east of Limerick city. Farming and estate management were high among his extraordinarily wide range of interests as I found when I eventually inherited his working library of about 2,000 volumes.

My nature has precluded me from continuing a long line of Bourkes, since I realised my true inclinations at an early age. These memoirs incorporate the history of this happy old home, which I determined to try and save on leaving London in 1964 with the devoted support of George, my lover for more than 42 years. A service engineer by profession, it was due to his brilliant ability and enthusiasm for the project, that we ultimately saved it from most inopportune sales, bulldozers and fires, against enormous odds. Recently it has been given the accolade of a Preservation Order by Limerick County Council.

After George's death in 1986, having never borrowed from a bank but quickly reinvested the proceeds from the flats we created,

I sold the place to tenants whom we liked, and kept the best flat for the rest of my life. The new owners continue to improve the grounds, gardens and woodlands with more than two hundred mature beech, ash and oak trees. A finely curved avenue is the approach that in the spring is ablaze with daffodils, followed by primroses, violets and bluebells. In fact Thornfields restored has become my memorial to George, and enabled me to make my special Thai Thornfields, south of Chiangmai, for George's successor, Na. Above all, the old place has given me the ultimate happiness there, so totally unexpected, of continuity in our beautiful little adopted daughter Sirilac, now ten years old.

Wellington remarked that he lost two of his best officers "through their damn wives", and Richard – who was not knighted until 1842 – often took half-pay to be at home with his wife "Betsy", to whom he was so devoted. She was frequently unwell, being a heavy lady, but was keenly aware of her family duties, especially the care of their eldest son John who was born weak and almost blind, though he lived to middle age and was given an annuity instead of his inheritance. She taught the children music, acknowledging its great importance and reward. Proof of her interest in botany, too, we found in a book of notes she kept when at government house at the Cape, with the pressed flowers still mostly intact.

In fact Thornfields quickly became an ideal secluded family residence for my ancestor, a devout, though liberal, Protestant. Right from the beginning, they built up an exemplary rapport with their tenants and neighbours, assisting them whenever possible with information or training. They knew the duties incumbent on those in a privileged position through good education, especially now owning a property near Castleconnell, so very long associated with the Bourke family.

The full extent of this vital close friendship came to light only a few years ago when our solicitors' office finally closed, and they suddenly found another family deed box, open I may add, and had the temerity to sort the contents before informing me of the discovery. "There's only one thing that may be important", they told me casually, "A manuscript by some well-known ancestor".

On top of numerous relevant papers they had laid an undamaged 40 pp. manuscript by Sir Richard, without a single correction, dated May 1831, entitled "A memorandum on leaving to assume the governorship of New South Wales". The impassioned document gave detailed instructions as to what he wanted done with his lands while he was away. Each holding shows what was to be assisted there and how the tenant was to be protected. For example he stated that poor widows were to be given help if prices increased, and no pressure was to be placed on those genuinely unable to meet their dues.

It is the outpouring of a man of compassion, which also marked his governor-ship in the ensuing years. Unfortunately his manager did not always live up to his duties, as was perhaps inevitable. But how very well we were rewarded by his actions that undoubtedly saved Thornfields in the troubled times far ahead. (A friend, Margaret Power from Castleconnell, has recently done her MA thesis on "General Sir Richard Bourke in his Time and Place".)

Not wishing to return from Australia "in half", as he expressed it, having left dear Betsy buried at Parramatta on the outskirts of Sydney only five months after their arrival, he chose to travel by a most circuitous route, calling at Fiji, then going up the Andes, across Argentina by mule, and finally leaving from Rio de Janeiro.

In 1825 before his travels abroad, he built a small school within his woods for seventy local children and was its active manager, with assistance from family members and the clergy. We found the list of rules for Ahane School, that being the name of the Catholic Church and a few small houses gathered there. "Equal tuition to both religions" stands proudly first among them. Furthermore there he was later able to instigate some important educational reforms impossible during his administration in Australia.

The school was used for more than a century until a national school was built further up the road. I can remember watching pupils playing happily in an area fenced off simply from the wood.

Sometimes parents would tell me how their own childhood had been greatly helped by attendance there. The Kildare Place Society gave a grant towards its construction.

Meanwhile Richard was busy editing the correspondence of Edmund Burke in co-operation with Lord Fitzwilliam, the first to do so. But soon the dreadful famine began to descend on all. Many extensions to Thornfields' grounds date from famine times when they tried to give extra employment; for example the acre of walled garden was capped with huge Liscannor flags, and much drainage was undertaken in the woodlands. He also commissioned extra Limerick furniture at the time, assisted emigration and even arranged soup kitchens in the basement when required.

He was on the bench of magistrates and became High Sheriff, whereas his closest personal friendship was with Lord Monteagle who lived further down the Shannon estuary at Mount Trenchard, and shared his interest in music. Soirées were often held in our formal drawing-room with gilt-wood pelmets surrounding a concert grand piano by Wieck of Dresden, the factory owned by Clara Schumann's father. (I discovered a diary kept then by a family member with the significant entry: "I hear talk of a young Polish pianist, Chopin. I wonder will he become any good"!)

Sir Richard's second son, Richard also, but known as Dick, who had been his secretary in Sydney, was sent back to study law at Lincoln's Inn in London. He wrote out "How terrible to be studying law in London fogs when I might instead by walking in Sydney's lovely botanical gardens". In due course he became a local government inspector and married Ann O'Grady of Kilballyowen, daughter of The O'Grady, and ran Thornfields efficiently through the second half of the 19th century dying in 1902, having continued to enjoy local esteem.

The governor "Fell asleep in this House of the Lord" in 1855, his memorial states in Stradbally Church, but he actually returned home briefly aged 78, and nearly blind. He was buried in a vault made by James Pain who designed cornices for Thornfields many years earlier. On seeing his father prepared, Dick described him lying there: "so calm and beautiful, so noble and open. Fair in death as in life".

Dick continued expanding crafts at their school and his wife being an excellent wood-carver, established "Ahane and Stradbally Carving School" where the skill was taught for many years. Her own ability is seen in lovely examples I retain, and the general standard was so high apparently that pieces made by the group are much sought after today. The family was also associated with establishing the Limerick "Mechanics Institute".

Meanwhile the farm became neglected, parts of the lands were sold, some given away and more was stolen since the governor was the last to be interested in farming. But the result of his work is still apparent, especially with trees such as a giant pair of cedars of Lebanon that stand like sentinels near the lawn.

The governor's daughter Anne, who had acted as hostess in Sydney after her mother's death, married the Colonial Secretary Deas Thomson and they had thirteen children. It was partly to accommodate the consequent flow of nephews and nieces from Australia on holiday that Richard decided to build on a wing in about 1865. Unlike the main house, it has no basement but is built about four feet above ground which allows excellent cross-ventilation. This is where I now have my lower wing flat with a very large drawing room that is in someways the best-proportioned room in the house. Three very large low windows with plate glass and internal pine shutters look out onto lawns, woods and an unusual white rhododendron.

My father, Richard too but known as Dick, was born in 1884, elder son of the governor's grandson John Ulick who was one of the first pupils at St. Columba's College. He became the first Irishman to row in the boat race for Cambridge in 1866 and '67, and founded the Limerick lawn tennis club in 1877, the year the Wimbledon championships began and the older Limerick boat club. Our only flurry of sportsmanship.

But alas his experience as an Irish resident magistrate was to die of drink when only 65, an occupational hazard one might imagine. As a consequence my father was a lifelong teetotaller, and Ulick remains a shadowy figure; he had married a Vandeleur from

Castleconnell, whose ancestor Colonel Vandeleur distinguished himself at Waterloo and wrote a memoir about the battle.

Unlike his forebears my father was not at all academically inclined, and left school early to study for a while at Crewe engineering works. But soon he set off instead to Africa where he was very lonely initially, but later became enraptured with the country, even to the extent of ever afterwards wearing riding breeches and puttees, though I never saw him near a horse. He stayed in Africa many years, mostly tea planting far inland from Durban, but he also worked briefly as an engineer at a gold mine. When tea planting he was sometimes fifty miles from the nearest white settler, yet found the isolation idyllic, despite frequent bad attacks of malaria and other illnesses that left him often unwell in later years.

His pastime was big game shooting, I regret to say, accompanied by his servants, who acted as retrievers. Proof of these exploits survive at Thornfields, among them a magnificent leopard skin, still flying up the staircase, that the best London taxidermist, Rowland Ward, declared the finest specimen they had ever prepared. But the poor beast left its mark, literally, on one of my father's legs. Crocodiles succumbed too, one with a bangle inside, my father told me, and antelope and even hippopotami were not spared.

While there he became very fond of one of his two black servants, Eldelama, of whom I still have a faded photograph showing a slim black lad of about 23 holding aloft some trophy from the forest. Shortly before his death in 1952 having been two years bedridden, partly from these exploits, he told me a strange story about this period in Africa.

During one of the many native uprisings – often the blacks were treated little better than slaves – Eldelama brought him a colt revolver which he had been given to shoot him with, but chose fortunately to surrender it instead. "I still have it" my father told me, much to my surprise since I had never seen it, until it turned up about three years ago, hidden under a floor-board in its original holster. So once again a bullet could so very easily have forestalled my life.

In gratitude, and because he greatly liked the lad, my father wanted to bring him back to Thornfields when he finally returned, had not his future mother-in-law put her foot down in abject horror at the idea. When I was young I used to see him take out cheaply made children's books about tigers and mongooses with which, no doubt, he once tried to teach the lad English.

The tale I find very sorrowful: I dare not think of their parting knowing that they would not be able to keep any contact in the future. It is occasions such as these that indelibly mark one's life, remain and fester; here was likely born his constant unwavering support of my chosen open gay life. What about his delighted expression when, aged about sixteen I chanced to name our new tri-colour cocker spaniel puppy "Pansy"? It was then too that he looked around sadly at the house, scarcely decorated this century and wished me luck if I could ever do anything with it.

Chapter two

Troubles Ahead

In 1912 my father leased Thornfields to Colonel Ribton Gore of the Royal Sussex Regiment, a genial stout man with a military moustache. In many ways his family was ideal for the lovely country residence that Thornfields had by then become, comprising his wife Ada, née Dendy, whom he married when she was only sixteen, four daughters and an only son, Gerard, a pupil at Cheltenham College, known perhaps inevitably as Ruddigore.

Ada, the eldest daughter, was apparently a self-appointed governess, martialing them to roll the lawn before breakfast with an iron roller intended for an ass. Not long after they settled in, however, Evelyn, aged about twenty and a talented artist, died of peritonitis. The other sisters were gentle Esmée, whose duty, as so often in those days, was to remain unmarried to look after her mother in her eventual long widowhood, almost as an unpaid servant, and Mabel Pauline, petite and loving whom I should have placed first since she became my father's 'beloved consort' - Haydn's music for her in "The Creation" is only adequate I feel - for thirty-three years, and my adoring mother. Never did I hear a harsh word, or see an unkind gesture between them, despite the great difficulties soon after their marriage during the Irish 'Troubles'.

The first two years of their tenancy resounded with laughter from tennis parties, often led by Gerard, their mother's declared favourite. The grounds were beautifully maintained since my father had leased the place reasonably on condition they continued to employ three outside staff in addition to the domestic servants. In the evening the older folk would take out the croquet set, and the solid clunks therefrom even resounded when I was put to bed at about six, not many years later.

All the Gores painted, well it seems to me, but they had the habit of a cuckoo mostly putting their efforts into frames that already contained works belonging to their landlord. For example on exploring behind one rather feeble effort, we found it was backed by a lovely pencil drawing of my great-grandmother's sister, Thomasina O'Grady, signed L. Wagner 1842; at least the intruder had protected it from light for some years. The family was also interested in photography, having a very wide-angled plate camera that we found along with much of their work, chiefly depicting tennis parties and leisurely Sundays on the lawn.

But alas my grandmother Ada Gore was rather a snob; one can see her playing the chatelaine in several photos, such as one of her grandly seated in a carriage at the front door. She had an elaborate family tree prepared, showing her husband's lineage in detail, as a branch of the Earl of Arran's family, taking it back to Alderman Gore, Lord Mayor of London in 1609, almost exactly 200 years after Dick Whittington. In her old age she even had a crest painted on her car, to my horror, and often sat grandly manipulating a pianola, such an instrument of deceit. (Recently I discovered the first Wimbledon winner was A.W. Gore; I cannot see him on her tree, and I hope the very ancient racquet we later threw out was not the one that won the day!)

I am uncertain as to my father's exact movements in the ensuing years, before he married my mother at Thornfields in 1918, but most of the time was spent back in Africa. Obviously his visits to Thornfields soon became much more than a duty of inspection, when he became so attached to Mabel, the quietest member of the family who for ever walked in awe of sister Ada.

The Gores presumably kept in touch with political developments through the regiment in Limerick, if not otherwise, but my father must have heard almost nothing in that line in his self-imposed exile. Native runners brought him occasional post, but Mabel's letters certainly did not

16

constitute general reportage.

But alas, these idyllic years were brief. After Evelyn's death, Gerard went off to join up in 1914 when still only 18 years old. Then on Christmas Eve our local postmistress saw to her horror that the post for Thornfields, mostly brightly decorated, included a sombre telegram from the war office, which by then she recognised only too well. Like most neighbours, she had found the Gores suitable tenants for old Thornfields, especially since the Colonel was Irish. What was she to do? Surely she acted correctly withholding the dreadful item until immediately after the festive season?

The local Catholic priest sought permission to hold a 'Requiem Mass' in Ahane church, immediately outside the estate wall, a kindly gesture my mother never forgot. And at once the lad's mother wore unrelieved black, even a neckband to the day she died in 1940 – surely Gerard would not have wished it so. She changed her pew in our church for a hidden position, thinking she was being stared at, and in her frenzied grief sent off for paper scrap to help the war effort a pile of 'old papers' from a special large pine chest, made for them. They included the original plans of Melbourne, and some of Clive's dispatches from India that happened to be temporarily stored there. What a terrible family loss, and an important historical one too. But against this, I recall her demented state even in 1937, when she looked aghast on hearing I was off to visit a German school. In 1964 it was left to me, it so happened, to gather up my namesake's Cheltenham books off a tilted shelf inside a mahogany inset glass-fronted bookcase in what is now my drawing-room, exactly 50 years after he had last used them. (Strange, I hope he would have approved the life I lead in his name).

Obviously the family watched the implications of the Easter Rising carefully, though papers would not have then been easily obtained at Thornfields, hidden in its wood. After the Gores left – except my dear mother – it soon became clear that Limerick was likely to become a centre of unrest.

On Labour Day 1918, 10,000 marched in general dissatisfaction in the city, and when in the following December, Sinn Féin won almost all the seats in Dáil elections this added even more concern, and the following year the Limerick demonstration became so fierce it was known as the "Limerick Soviet".

Meanwhile Thornfields began to decline once the Gores left since my parents had no regular income whatsoever, and my father's ill-health precluded him from seeking work. Instead he hoped to continue working the walled garden, albeit with one man only. Similarly we were reduced to two servants, or one at times, to maintain the enormous house; the wing was unused except to receive broken furniture and such. My parents were completely disinterested in politics, but would have voted Fine Gael, if at all.

Luckily my father saw he had only one option, to be strictly neutral in the local terror. The house was basically unlocked anyhow, and whoever called was told to take what they saw which would have been but little. It was then that my family's happy relations with the neighbours paid such handsome dividends. Local people came to my father's defence when any danger seemed particularly imminent. Once a machine-gun was placed on top of the porch during some alarm.

My sister Evelyn was born February 20th 1920, just as the troubles increased. Also about that time, when my mother was returning on her bicycle from the post she was shouted at: "Lie down, Miss!" while an ambush took place overhead. How terrified she must have been. Then three months later a close friend of hers, Winifred Barrington, daughter of Sir Charles Barrington of Glenstal Abbey, now the premier Catholic boys' school up in the hills behind Thornfields, was shot dead while returning from a fishing trip to Newport with an officer among the party in her car. "That'll teach you to associate with the British", she was told while dying.

Some hope seemed to appear late in 1921 however, when Lloyd George and Michael Collins signed the Anglo-Irish Treaty on December 7th, three days before I arrived as a 'harbinger of peace'. I hope to see another. I happened to find my mother's diary for that period; entries are few – what time had she to be a diarist? – but dramatic. "Gerard weighs 8 lbs." is followed by "Annacotty Bridge blown up"; thereby cutting the Limerick-Dublin road a mile away; next is written, "Bought a ton of coal. £1" And over the pages comes "War in Limerick" in the following July.

The struggle for Limerick in fact became a turning point in the civil war when 700 republican troops took over the barracks. It was then, mirabile dictu, that a canon last used in 1691 was fired, partially, from King John's Castle at a barracks across the Shannon. In fact the recoil defeated those who tried to induce it to resume its fearful duties. Provincial troops ultimately won the city after two days' fierce fighting and much destruction in the centre. A final engagement took place at Kilmallock 25 miles away.

Understandably this was all too much for my parents to bear especially when they awoke one morning to find two graves dug in front of the house with their names thereon. This treacherous act, they later discovered, had been done by the remaining gardener hoping to rob the house at his leisure.

Also not long before they had found a ghastly notice hanging in the yard saying: "This place will be burned to the ground tonight!" They hurriedly sent my sister, then about three years old, to the care of neighbours, and cradled me, I imagine, in their arms. Luckily sufficient of our protectors from nearby must have been alerted to forestall the fearful act.

Soon afterwards they decided regretfully to try and sell the house and its contents; where they could have gone or what they intended to do I cannot imagine. Recently I saw the 1923 advertisement in "The Limerick Leader". Demand must have been minimal, and they knew absolutely nothing about the value of the important items in their possession. Eventually a convent showed interest in acquiring the place, but the Order withdrew its offer when it discovered it was, in their restricted view, a Protestant house!

The implications of this strange decision were enormous for me, when no other buyer surfaced. Without the house and its contents which my father hoped would all come to me, I might well now be old and paupered in a country, furthermore, that pays no non-contributory old age pensions, among the Friday free-for-all, despite the fact that one has always paid indirect taxation, to anyone with a minimum of assets.

So in this way my parents were forced to stay on at Thornfields with their young children in very difficult circumstances, which were never expressed in any way to us as we grew older. They were completely isolated, with only our Nanny, dear old Mary from a village near Nenagh, and the gardener who had to spend most of his time cutting wood, or pumping up water from the very deep well by hand. Even when large trees fell it was difficult to cut them up alone in the days of two-handed cross-saws. The overgrown laurel paths provided an easier source of wood, and being a fruitwood, it burns very well. (Into these at night came many thousands of starlings to roost, fortunately they now have chosen to slumber elsewhere.)

There was only the basement kitchen, and a bathroom distant in the top wing flat. Thermos flasks were much used I imagine to retain hot water for us children and my father's endless cups of tea, strong and black, a legacy from planting it. We kept fowl, which pleased the many foxes hidden in the laurels; badgers chose to emerge at night and dig up the lawn, not that it mattered with on-one to maintain it properly. Night-time must have been terrifying. Oil lamps and blackened silver candlesticks sent weird lights flickering in the gloom. All the paintwork was dark brown. What if fire broke out, or anyone suffered an accident or sudden bad illness. Daytime was better; our nanny took us to the railway bridge over the Dublin line, as was noted – once to our delight, the train driver threw a box of chocolates onto the embankment.

The garden provided produce though its formal paths, lined with forget-me-nots and London Pride, quickly deteriorated. But the bed of huge dahlias remained where I hunted caterpillars. There were many fruit trees, quinces, and black, red and white currants and gooseberries too, if our red-setter chose to leave us any. My mother also grew colourful cinerarias and calceolarias in the unheated conservatory, and richly scented hyacinths in the drawing room in the winter months.

Once a week my parents went in shopping, and my father – who would never be driven – was angry if 'his' place outside our grocers was already taken. While my mother shopped modestly, my father would walk up two blocks to see his solicitor, for a rest really; the subject did not matter. He certainly did not realise that he was thereby spending, in the long term, far more than my mother, since the firm had the odious habit, but very profitable, of only sending bills to the deceased who were unlikely to contest them, and incidentally charging twice if two subjects had been mentioned.

It was only after his death in 1952 that this came to light, when I was presented, on behalf of my mother, with a two-volume bill of costs. Unfortunately at the time I had never heard of the statute of limitations which would have enabled me to cross out many of the older entries. (Though I am told it is very difficult to find a solicitor to support you in this matter, especially in Limerick where they frequently refuse to act against each other.)

Our only friends at the time, apart from Willie Howley OSI who owned Rich Hill, a suitably named adjacent estate, and was once high in the Indian civil service, were a duo of Canons, with two daughters each our age. Canon Davis, a very lame widower, was in charge of our family Stradbally church, whereas Canon Westropp lived with his amiable wife at Kilmurry. Doubtless they knew as little about Irish politics as did my father, so we were completely secluded, and excluded by lack of money. We never once ate in a restaurant, other than a tea, that I can recall.

Yet my early years were blissfully happy; I saw the perfect love between my parents which endured all their lives, and I fully understood when my mother took her own life ten years after my father's death, wanting no more misery alone without even television for company.

In one of the earliest photos of me with her a jar of worms is by my side, and all my early forays were for fishing or shooting at my father's instigation. He taught me to fly-fish for trout to such effect that one day when 13 years old I caught 60 at the upper Clare Glen, named after the Earls of Clare.

When I was about six I was sent to Miss Fogarty's kindergarten school in Limerick, having had a governess very briefly, whom I once startled by writing about a five-page essay instead of the few lines my sister offered. Indeed one of my earliest memories is of trying to decide with which hand to write being so totally ambidextrous.

Miss Fogarty, a smiling lady about 50, had her school firstly in Barrington's Street, but soon after I joined we moved to the smart "Landsdowne House" on the Ennis Road. There were about twenty children learning there; our father used to drive us in mostly, but sometimes we shared the journeys with the local canons. If by chance we arrived late, the illogical punishment was to be given lines of verse to learn; the harder I tried the more impossible it became, yet how very easily music is recalled.

My favourite subject was mathematics. Learning tables became quick fun, and before I left her charming little school I used to test myself by finding how quickly I could solve all her problems stored away in a cardboard box. She was much surprised by my fascination. They say music is allied to maths and I can recall the afternoon I crouched outside the classroom while the girls danced waltzes she played on an old piano, my very first and exhilarating encounter with music.

We sometimes went for short holidays to stay with my father's severely crippled younger sister Slaney, whom he adored, at Dunmore East. She had been on crutches all her adult life, and was as tall as he, about six feet two. At The Bungalow, then a distinctive name, she would lie on a couch on the lawn and wave to passers-by, all of whom knew her well.

There doubtless were girls on Councillors' Strand, but I only noticed boys; one summer when I was about eight I only had eyes for a ginger-haired lad of ten, little knowing why. Later I thought of trying to go to sea, a masculine world, like my cousin Bill Anderson planned to do, but oddly enough I thought only boys who lived by the sea, as he did, would be accepted.

During these years we grew our own vegetables and fruit and my father sometimes managed to sell excess produce such as strawberries, gladioli, and seakale to corner shops, even lettuce painstakingly watered.

My early days were inevitable lonely, but it would have been considered incorrect for me to go and help with the local harvests.

The only altercation I recall with my sister was when she dared to put on a boy's shirt and tie one morning; my orientation strongly objected to the sight. She was interested chiefly in horses and later went foxhunting, having to hack as far as Four Elms to do so. I considered it far too dangerous and cruel, but would gladly shoot foxes instead, or exercise her hunter on the road.

Visitors very seldom called at Thornfields. If they did my mother would rush to try and assemble an adequate tea. The beautiful old drawing room was scarcely ever used; its gilt pelmets were festooned with cobwebs; although we quickly had a bamboo plantation after my father had brought a small piece down from Glenstal to make a screen behind which I could shoot pigeons, no-one ever thought of making a long-reaching broom, so much more important.

But when I recall the little songbirds I shot almost daily with my airgun, during holidays, I am utterly appalled. I can hardly write about it. For example there was a prunus tree outside my father's study – a misnomer since he never did so – and the bullfinches ate the buds, to his horror. It was my duty to kill as many as possible of these lovely creatures. I never stopped to think how much more beautiful they were than the flowers. I had no mercy for my prey, and it became worse when I was lent a .410 shogun; rabbits fell around me, and later woodcock and snipe, since I became an excellent shot- at least I could eat those victims. (Other boys were shooting goals at football; I was taking lives.) This continued until when I was about 24 my lover George saw me shoot a cock pheasant, and at once brought me to my senses. "Couldn't we buy one already dead?" He pleaded, and I never shot again.

The most vivid holiday I remember from my young days was a week in a rented flat at Ballybunion, Co. Kerry. At night passing revellers vomited over the low wall in front of the house; but by day my father taught me to swim, tied to a rope, pulling me across rock pools when the tide was low.

I made friends with a lively young black boy – almost the first I had ever seen – aged about ten, with whom I wandered through deep meadows chasing butterflies, such as we see no longer, alas, blown in by Atlantic gales. The lad whom my father liked, though so very much younger than his Eldelama, was the son of an elderly man with a temporary shooting gallery near the castle ruin. I wept when saying good-bye to my little friend, to face more loneliness at home.

Chapter three

At Aravon Prep School

From the age of nine until thirteen, I was sent to Aravon preparatory school at Bray, Co. Wicklow, probably because it was then considered the best such school, but also because the headmaster, Arthur Craig, had unfortunately been a friend of my father who had been the school's first registered pupil in about 1895 when it was founded by "Old Bookey", a family friend. (T.P. Watts actually taught us both.) The headmaster was tall, about 50, with a prominent nose, and a moustache that predated Hitler's. He soon became the only person in my life that I would most gladly have seen

drop dead at my feet. I can still feel the swing of the sidecar that took my father and I on the too short journey to the school from Bray station, with my wooden tuck-box loaded with large pears from our garden, perched as balance to us both.

The school itself was a pretty building in pleasant grounds enclosed by a high stone wall, and there was ample space for sport training essential to the régime. The first term my father left me there sadly, after asking the prettiest pupil he saw to take care of me. After he left, other youngsters were dragged screaming from cars by their parents. I had arrived for four years education in a school run by an ever-unsmiling tyrant. There were then about 40 boarders and 5 day boys.

In his defence I can only say he had evidently seen his twin brother shot beside him in the first world war, and was injured himself, having a metal plate inserted under his left cheek that sweated profusely when he raged. He himself taught maths which fortunately I understood well for my age; but also French, making us learn by rule of thumb – and out of terror- never once suggesting we might one day need the language for work or holidays.

On my first evening, I dropped a sandwich, probably from nerves, and was promptly given a lecture on hunger in the Far East, and the millions that would have enjoyed the humble offering. Pocket money we deposited with him, being given imitation bank withdrawal books to teach us thrift, or caution. Later I discovered that if given five shillings when visiting my aunt Esmée at her home nearby, the best plan was to bury it like a dog, in a flower-bed, watching the brute did not see my action, and excavate it later when needed.

"You awful fool of a boy!" Craig would cry, when some boy mispronounced a word, or was slow at maths, and immediately slap him hard across the face almost causing him to fall off the groggy desk. He never assaulted me, possible because of his former friendship with my father, but once I did receive three hard strokes of his cane, kept in a cupboard in his study for not understanding some advanced arithmetic, after missing a week from illness. What a strange way to improve ability, I thought; my cousin Bill he often hit hard, to my horror, since he was not very bright.

Our sports were cricket played at a very large ground the school owned near the middle of Bray, long since overbuilt and rugby in the winter. Soccer was considered too common a sport, but I think I would have much preferred it as a less fierce alternative, from the few games I did manage to enjoy. There was fortunately a hard tennis court in the garden where I quickly improved at my chosen sport. It was a wonder that Craig did not forbid me playing in my totally ambidextrous manner.

But I was a disaster at cricket, Craig's favourite sport, since I could not throw the ball the length of a room or bowl into the correct practise net so round-armed was I. Yet I was lined up with other boys while Craig belted cricket balls at us, and gloated when our fingers were hurt, or we dropped the wretched missile. I enjoyed watching cricket matches, however, if I had a suitable partner on my rug, usually slightly younger than myself. Sometimes I kept the scores safely ensconced within the pavilion.

One day at rugby poor Medlicott managed to break the touch-judge flag, caught somehow between his knees, and Craig wildly ranted and raved at him, such puerile behaviour. The field was ten minutes walk from the school, and I have always regretted that I did not have the courage towards the end of my stay to walk into the police station we passed, adjacent to the school, to report the evil man directly. I considered it seriously. What restrained me only was the thought that a 12-year-old would not be believed, and my father would then have had to remove me next day from Craig's insane wrath. Another time I wondered what I might put in his food hopefully to give us a respite for some weeks.

In the dining hall, for example, a boy would have to walk with Craig's cup of tea from a distant urn, and if one drop was spilt en route it was enough to fire off another verbal torrent. At the bottom table with the youngest boys sat Miss Walshe, "Squelch", a stout lady who wore pince-nez, a kindly matron who was a badly needed refuge at moments of distress. She dried our hair on her ample lap after baths, or wiped away a tear. Once she had the terrible task of telling a friend of mine that his brother had been killed on his motorbike, coming out to see him.

We had a scout troop well organised by Mr. Hughes, the art master, a genial man prone to gout, who could immediately draw the most fantastic birds on request, even on a cigarette packet, to my delight. I learned from him one very important lesson, too, the irrelevance of impartiality. He was leaving, to my regret, and as he entered his last few classes he brought in small gifts, little silver items included, showing them to the class and giving each to my cousin Bill, a year younger than I, with his mass of blond curls. I understood at once he must be his pet, and thought, why not? We cannot truthfully like everyone equally, and it is much more honest to show partiality.

One term Craig summoned the school together to declare he had found two boys in bed together, and that he was determined to exorcise such filth. All 40 boys – apart from me it seemed – were summoned to his study singly to 'burn their boats' and tell him all they knew of sex!

On scouting trips we often went to Powerscourt grounds, or Kilruddery, and I still remember the thrill, and terror, of a boy I liked especially sitting me on the handlebars of his bike, and racing down a hill with me in that perilous position. I remember too during my last days there seeing beautiful Honan sitting alone on a bench reading in the sun with his hair falling in disarray. But to balance that, ugly Kelleher, placed next to me in the sick-bay, chose to explore beneath my bedclothes rather to my dismay – an event that he, not I, had obviously forgotten when we met in Trinity some years later.

My stay at Aravon ended dramatically. I had sat for a scholarship for entrance to St. Columba's College at Rathfarnham in the Dublin mountains, and heard early in the summer term of 1936 that I had been awarded a scholarship of £30 a year for four years, not an insignificant sum in those days, especially for my father. He came up, staying at the Standard Hotel as usual since that was as far as he dared drive in the fast Dublin traffic. We walked down to St. Stephen's Green, which was all he could manage through illness, and then to my utter delight he suddenly told me there, as we passed a colourful display of summer flowers, that he had come to take me home. I was to leave Aravon at last: I could have danced on every wallflower in delight. He had taken the logical view that since I had won the scholarship it seemed unnecessary to force me to stay on for the rest of the summer term at Aravon - the name was from Novara Road, inverted like its headmaster.

Apparently he raged, as usual, at the news, how it would upset his other pupils – but not his expenses I presumed. No music had been heard in the junior prison except when we were marched in a crocodile to Bray Cathedral every Sunday wearing horrible straw hats laughed at by lucky lads with freedom to go into shops and buy sweets. But as I gradually heard the singularly beautiful cathedral bells, a clarion responded deeply within me. Otherwise there were only certain afternoons when an aged lady came to give piano lessons to about six pupils. How I wished it might have been me, yet I could not ask my father to pay out extra on my education.

I merely sat within earshot, enduring some awful pupil gaffes.

Oddly enough we learned to play bridge there among ourselves; I suppose cards were allowed since we had no money possibly to deter some boys from trying to escape, as happened about every six months. The railway line, in sight, was an added enticement. There were "dinky toys" to race in the high old gym building, where heavy curtains hung, and were sometimes shaken in the mornings to yield moths for examination. The vaulting horse was an added instrument of torture, especially if Craig was nearby.

Some years later a lady in Limerick telephoned me to ask if the horror stories her younger son was telling her about Aravon could possibly be true, causing him to be so very unhappy. I told her most certainly they were. She could probably double them.

It hurts in retrospect to have seen Bill Anderson abused - never in the sexual connotation – that at least we were mercifully spared. He came from such a tragic family. My father's older sister Aileen married Paul Anderson, a rich gentleman who had a superb house and farmlands at Glasshouse, Mount Prospect, on the bank of the river that flows from Waterford to the sea. Lawns sloped down to the river, and large ships went by; greetings were waved from on board. At the foot of the lawns was the railway, too, where a very occasional train passed sedately by.

I stayed there happily, and was sometimes taken out on their yacht. Bill was utterly spoilt as an only child swathed in excess clothing. His parents were a delight, and very popular locally with many discreet kindnesses to their credit.

But then disaster struck. Uncle Paul dropped dead in his Waterford club when only about 55, and Bill volunteered for submarines in the war, and was soon reported lost. My father went down to try and comfort his sister, formerly so very bright and cheerful. (At Aravon she once astonished me by remarking: "Gerry, what beautiful hands you have", and later encouraged my attempts to write poetry.) But only a year later my father had to return there since poor Aileen had thrown herself under the daily train, ostensibly trying to save her lost son's dog.

My father was shattered by the news, and returned here to

bed, scarcely leaving it again. He had naturally placed her closest friend, a Miss Power, in the front pew, knowing she was Catholic. But Bishop Harvey, who was conducting the service, approached her and asked her to move to the back of a Protestant church – so I first encountered bigotry at its very worst.

Shortly before I left Aravon, much to our surprise Craig became engaged to a large lady about his age called Esther. To celebrate the event, doubtless on her instigation, they took five of us senior boys to the Gaiety theatre to see "The Mikado" in his open char-a-banc like car. Naturally I was delighted with what I saw and heard, and sang softly "Three little maids from school" and other catchy tunes to myself for the rest of the term. That, and winning a medal in an airgun shooting competition, is about my sole happy memory – not much to garner from four years at my hated prep school. But at least it had prepared me well academically for St. Columba's, that I immediately enjoyed in sharpest contrast.

Incidentally, while at Aravon I first became interested in flies – trout flies that is – used for wet-fly fishing, after Reggie Fitzmaurice, my father's closest friend there some 35 years earlier, who still visited Thornfields quite often, called and brought me a kit for tying them. I tried to copy the well-known "Greenwell's Glory", "Blue Dunn", and the "Devil" (alias A.B. Craig). Included was a small vice, used to hold the hooks, the only one ever permitted in that horrid juvenile prison.

Chapter four

St. Columba's College

After Aravon I was sent to St. Columba's College above
Rathfarnham in the foothills of the Dublin Mountains overlooking
the bay. It was then the only Protestant public school in southern
Ireland, and a sister-school of Radley in England. There were 120
boys at it, and girls had not yet been admitted.

I escaped Aravon's horrendous régime with great delight, and
in free time on my first afternoon I went for a walk up the mountains, gorse covered high up, offering superb views on clear days,
with Hurley from Sandycove, whom I chose as the best-looker of
those seemingly free for a stroll. Odd, since we were soon to
become academic twins for the four years lying ahead, both special-
ising in experimental science; he was my pace-setter, usually a mark
or two above me, and always adjacent therefore on the school roll-
call. As a final insult, he beat me into third place for a sizarship to
Trinity, during examinations for which I stayed with him and his
widowed mother at Sandycove. Our friendship ended abruptly,
however, shortly before I left, when I told him I was gay, at least in
thought if all too seldom in deed. "How terrible! You'll end up a
dirty old man", was his ill-tempered ignorant retort; I hope he

learned compassion in later life, possibly from his two older barrister brothers. His own life ended as an atomic scientist in America – happy I hope.

My first year at St. Columba's was too easy academically, as I realised, since I was placed among youngsters of the same age but significantly less qualified not having been subjected to my frightening early education. Most classes I enjoyed —especially getting 100% on a 'Common Entrance' maths paper – but art lessons I greatly disliked being unable to draw, and because the master adopted the stupid method, if such it was, of merely showing you prints of famous paintings and sneering at your inability to name them.

On the other hand I enjoyed English, except for the fact that I was allowed to read Shakespeare aloud without ever being told to observe the punctuation at the end of lines. No wonder the rubbish that flowed did little justice to the Bard. Once a new English master noting my facility with words - George noted I was "gullible and voluble" – commented "Bourke if I could write like you, I'd be a writer."

We did not specialise until halfway through our stay at S.C.C., and then I chose mathematics, and science which we were taught by George Lodge, a pleasant elderly widower often humming the "Miserere" from 'Il Trovatore' in memory of his dear wife. His lectures I found logical and interesting. Once I was deeply stung when the headmaster Rev. C.W. Sowby summoned me to his study to inform me I wrote up my experiments in bad English, a criticism I thought grossly unfair.

Sowby was about 55, portly, very fair-headed, and rather red-faced. I gathered much later that he was unpopular with his staff. An interesting example of this came when he summoned the school together to inform us of the great perils of masturbation. The giggling offenders were a few hours later discreetly informed by the three house masters that such rubbish was in the head's mind not theirs. "Carry on boys", they summarised.

George White was my benign house master and later an author of a history of the school. He taught Latin chiefly, and was genial and very fair-minded. He even kept a secret card index of his opinion of boys in his house so as to be prepared for truthful references in due course. I ultimately became Head of his Grange house so was much in contact with him, and delighted in his final summary of my days spent there. "Gerry works hard, without being brilliant, and has developed a very strong interest in music. He never lets cares weigh him down, and gets considerable joy out of life". Did he have a crystal ball, I wonder? If he ever saw two boys walking with arms entwined, especially before examinations, he would say: "Go on, kiss and get it over."

He appointed me a prefect when I was about 17, but sent me a letter saying he had one reservation about me which was that he feared I was a 'yes-man' – why not be a real individual? I was momentarily hurt by the missive, but it changed my life in a flash. Forthwith I decided to take as my personal motto Polonius' advice to Laertes in "Hamlet": "This above all to thine own self be true!" The following year he called me "resolute in action", evidently seeing a transformation. (Fifty years later I heard he was still alive in Dublin, and asked him to lunch to thank him for his vital advice. His young teacher wife was almost in tears to hear a pupil do so; but he fully deserved the honour.)

During my 'teens at S.C.C. I enjoyed testing myself, not in athletics, which I hated, but in difficult situations. The most testing was my acceptance of Sowby's invitation to go down to Dublin, an almost unheard of treat during term time, to give a talk to the girls at Alexandra College. Knowing already how ill at ease I was with ladies, I thought it would be a real test of my development. I forget the subject, except that I ended by advising them to hurry home and listen to some Beethoven symphony due on the radio, and carried it out with élan, watched furthermore by Betty Farran, sister of a school friend, who was my nominal girl friend at the time, until she tried to kiss me, to my horror, while listening to the "Emperor Concerto" by moonlight. I suppose that had rather asked for it: not even the "Moonlight Sonata"?

Until you were a prefect you had to play compulsory games. Luckily I adored tennis, which I later played occasionally for Munster when about 19. There were two hard courts, and a masters' grass court to which I was often invited to show my strange ambidextrous play. I was captain of the tennis team, and playing a match at Portora was the only occasion in which I entered Northern Ireland, oddly enough. I was horrified then to hear the boys discuss at tea only which shops were Catholic or Protestant.

In the winter terms I was bound to play rugby since I had stupidly become good at it and played in almost every position, even fullback, at times. I ended up leader of the forwards when I grew heavier, but earlier had enjoyed the wing position being relatively fast. Yet I never played a game of rugby that I would not have preferred to miss, as on the occasion when I had to leave a radio relay of Mozart's "The Marriage of Figaro" in a master's rooms, to change for rugby in torrential rain. Furthermore I suffered terribly from chilblains all my 'teens, and rugby boots were instruments of torture. Sometimes I even had an arm in a sling when they were at their worst. Fortunately I left them behind me there.

Now to the evening I remember most vividly from my four years at S.C.C. It was October, and a new boy came late having been ill. He answered to the name of Wright with a startlingly beautiful "Yes, sir!" And when I looked over, being nearly 17, I saw Billy for the first time. He had jet-black hair, was of medium height and beamed an adorable smile. I fell in love on sight; you read of it in books, but I have been honoured to experience it three times to my amazement. Unfortunately no one can command it, or persuade it to enter one's scene. It is pre-ordained, and must be followed and obeyed.

Billy was a year younger than I, and our attraction was immediately mutual. We at once became inseparable, except during class, and unfortunately he was not in my house, so I could never share his dormitory. His initials were W.A.W. and "Wa-wa" he soon became. To this day I cannot pass a shop called Wright without a suddenly yearning for him. Our first walk together happened by chance; I had gone alone one way round Marley golf course and he alone around the other way. Bang, we coalesced and sped off united in happiness. I still feel the intensity. .

Of course other boys soon noticed we were always together

34

in our breaks; he was not very bright, and some classes lower. But he usually sat in a pew opposite me in the school chapel where we worshipped for half-an-hour morning and evening. Every time I looked to him he was looking to me, that same soft smile embellishing his lovely face. I adored him, and still do though I know not where he lives, or if he's alive. He could contact me if he chose. His name is not listed among old Columbans; naturally I have checked.

We walked every path and woodland up the mountain and lay in the long grass silently; love conquers chatter. But he never took my hand, or let me put it on his shoulder except once, when larking about in the showers I kicked him as he put down his elbow and broke my second toe completely backwards. Only then could I put my arm around his shoulder as I hobbled down to the sanatorium – a fair compensation for the accident.

"Gerry, if you ever marry, you'll marry a boy!" the oracle suddenly declared one day, adding that he could see no possible pleasure from playing around with another guy sexually. I heard someone more adventurous than I had once made a pass at him and been rewarded with a black eye. My best moment, surely came when I gave Billy a heavy tackle in a school rugby game and the master referee called out loudly: "Ah, the lovers' kiss that hurts but is desired"!

One holiday my father found me crying, and I admitted it was because I was not with Billy – he never visited Thornfields, I regret to say. Twice I stayed the night at Ulverton Road, Dalkey, where Dr.Wright lived with his family. We had twin beds, and I scarcely slept; the magnetism flowed in one direction only. Next day I watched from Kingstown pier with his mother as Billy and his father set off in their 27' racing yacht "Geraldine", on board which he never once invited me. "Gerry, you do love my Billy don't you?" said his Mum, as we watched nearby, noticing my sadness as the boat sailed slowly away.

The only prize I won at S.C.C. was for reading the lessons in chapel. One boy asked a master why I did not do it every day, as they liked my diction – but Billy and another favourite Charlie Graham were usually winking at me, trying to undermine the task.

Charlie, what memories he evokes. He was by far the best-looking new boy one September being blond, petite and with a curious habit of wandering around reading with a thin kisscurl dangling from his forehead. He came from St. Asaph, north Wales. I remember the address well since it was on some thirty letters I received from him after we separated that I kept in a fat bundle for many years. Innocuous, but from my second favourite while at St. Columba's. Alas, it had been left to an ugly prefect, later a clergyman, to initiate me during a walk up the mountain, amid a clump of gorse. I disliked his exploration, especially when he threatened to beat me up if I told anybody; yet the next year, when 15, I would not have minded a repeat performance.

The inevitable way ahead was eased by my friendship with D.F.L. "Dumpy" West, the little siren who told me he invariably seduced his sister's boyfriends before they reached her, was a protégé, too, of a well-known racing driver who would sometimes call to take him out on Sundays to old Sowby's horror. Once, to my disgust, he even asked me to spy on Dumpy and tell him who he was talking to – a suppressed gay, himself, perhaps?

Dumpy slept two beds away from me, among about 14 in the dormitory I was in charge of as a prefect; after lights-out I would often chat to him quietly, and at last I received my first full kiss from him. Although only 15, he immediately told me it was "perfectly natural", being well trained, no doubt. We used to swim together, naked, as was the rule, in the college outdoor swimming pool fed by a mountain stream. But, alas, he met a terrible end in 1965, when his white Rolls Royce failed to take a bend at Kildimo, Co. Limerick and he was killed outright while other lads were injured.

One master was a poet, and had three volumes published before being killed at the outset of the war. When I tried my hand at verse it must have been my mathematical streak that insisted I try sonnets. I doubt I had read many of Shakespeare's, and none of my youthful attempts survive. If not with my favourite, I preferred to walk alone, a characteristic I retain, and used to roam off to see how much more dog-roses had opened overnight, or any other gentle seasonal changes.

But the more I think of St. Columba's the more I think of Billy. I suppose he was correct never to acquiesce to holding hands, but it was a strange case of unrequited love, lasting so strongly for about three years. I even wanted to wear his clothes. Later I waited a whole afternoon for him to appear at my rooms in Trinity, watching for him to enter the main courtyard below.

Later in London he spent one Christmas during the war on leave from the navy in the small flat I had been lent in Chelsea; we ate reconstituted egg, but that mattered not at all with him. What, too, of the occasion when someone, I never discovered who, laid "Sweet William" flowers at my place in the dining hall in tribute to my friend. Ultimately he, too, became a prefect and George White told me, to my pleasure, that it was my influence on him that had earned him the position. I last saw Billy the week before I met George in London, and shortly afterwards someone sent me a cutting from "The Tatler" showing him in uniform – with a bride.

My parents wrote very regularly to me while I was at S.C.C. and I wrote home weekly as I was taught correctly at Aravon, a habit I gladly continued until their deaths. In one letter, when I was about 17, my father enclosed a photograph from a newspaper showing a beautiful lad, about my age, reclining at peace, in a deckchair, with no comment about it at all; the message was clear – nice, isn't he? I thought it a lovely simple gesture from my dear father, who must himself have grieved for his friend, Eldelama, at times.

Another test I subjected myself to: the headmaster asked when I was 15, who would like to go on an exchange visit to a German school at Spandau in Berlin for about six weeks. Six of us volunteered including Hurley, and we set off from Cobh to Hamburg on the liner "America" without any master escort. During the voyage I saw Cossack dancing for the first time, and one evening went right up inside the prow of the ship alone as it rose and fell dramatically in the heavy swell. Some boys became seasick, I just became hungrier.

We landed at Hamburg and went on by train to Spandau to the school where my pocket money of £7 was going to prove grossly inadequate; food was very meagre, including great hunks of hard bread hiding German sausages. Sometimes I put extra ones in my pockets in case of need ahead. On my first night, noticing the dormitory was very large with beds significantly touching side by side in pairs, my expectations were raised. But alas my luck was to be given a bed end-to-end along another wall.

Their soccer team had just won some competition and they took us out celebrating at a nearby bar. In their generosity they invited us to try some of each colourful item from the shelves behind. Alas I did so in youthful ignorance and reeled back to the school completely drunk. Soon I was violently sick into the sheets, and did not dare tell anyone next day, and endured the foul wrappings for several nights. I have never since dared to become drunk.

One American boy staying there told me he was not allowed to join in any games until his German was perfect – I was not even studying the language unfortunately. We were taken to Potsdam to see Frederick the Great's palace, and also to Dresden by bus. But the night for me was when we were taken to the Berlin State Opera on the Unter den Linden to see "The Flying Dutchman". I looked in the programme and wondered who Wagner might be. But once the curtain rose I was absolutely overwhelmed by the great seascape, the glorious music, the wonderful singing. "The sea rushes out wherever you open the score", commented an early conductor of Wagner's great early work, and indeed it did right into my lap on that fateful night.

Afterwards we were taken to a beer-hall; I did not admit to my thorough dislike of beer. The other boys laughed and chatted unconcernedly, ignoring completely what we had just witnessed. But I was utterly knocked out by the experience, and could only be left wondering when and how it might ever be repeated. So began my great love of music, all in one night, having heard none at home.

At the school we had to salute cleaners with "Heil Hitler" it being 1937, and we heard marching troops outside singing the Horst Wessel song, and other patriotic tunes during torchlight parades. That was the year, too, when Hitler had Gen. Röhm shot with a boyfriend by his side – events were moving fast politically, and in my own development.

Back at S.C.C. I told my music master what I had heard. He had a brochure of the Wagner festivals at Bayreuth on his door, so I presumed he was interested. From then on I visited his rooms frequently to play his records including Beethoven's fifth symphony and the superb fourth piano concerto – the work still evokes the smell of Groocock's cat's tray – and they soon became my closest allies at school. The slow movement of Mozart's clarinet concerto was also there, in poor condition, but the perfect discovery since no music is finer, despite its sad outpouring.

On the last side of Beethoven's fifth was the finale of Haydn 88th symphony marvellously witty sparkling music, and I thought how on earth could anyone write so many. In fact he composed 104, and I began listening to any of them on the radio, seeking one I did not enjoy, or could not understand. The search continues to this day.

I could only hear the radio in a master's rooms, or at home, since we were not allowed to possess one, though the school ironically had a radio club for assembling them. I persuaded a boy to lend me his hidden marvel, and lay in a loft in the yard the following year to hear Mozart's "Don Giovanni" from Glyndebourne knowing I'd be beaten if found, and have never enjoyed it more in hundreds of encounters.

But soon Joseph Groocock, our precentor, sympathised with my predicament and gave me music lessons for a few terms on the piano – no other instrument was then taught there. He also rashly promised to play me Mozart piano sonatas on request, and often kept his word. After services in our chapel I would hurry back to ask him what he had just played as a voluntary, since I quickly became knowledgeable on the subject.

Prefects changed for games in their dormitories, not in the general changing rooms. This I considered not a privilege but a disadvantage for obvious reasons, as the shower scene after games seemed the only justifiable reward for such ferocious exercise. Yet today I put my relative well-being, touch-wood, down to frequent exercise at school especially my daily tennis in the summer months at school or at home, and fast cycling up and down the mountains.

It was well worth walking up the heights above Tibradden or Ticknock to freewheel down the twisting roads.

Up there somewhere lived W.B. Yeats' wife at the time, and their son Michael was a colleague of mine – he did not like us reminding him of his father's poem that began: "Bid a strong ghost stand at the head that my Michael may sleep sound . . ." A descendant of J.M. Synge was also there and was a very solitary lad, introspective and calm.

Meanwhile at home my mother always chose my clothes for either school or home wear. I was utterly disinterested in my attire, and to this day prefer other people to decide for me. I take the view that I do not see what I myself am wearing. The choice was always George's prerogative, and now my Na's. How lucky that I had lovers with such very good colour senses.

In the holidays I had to go to dances unfortunately, with my sister in private homes, dance halls, or even hunt-balls occasionally. I hated them roundly, especially the terribly smoky atmosphere that used to send me sometimes dashing alone to the car outside with my sensitive eyes streaming with tears. Occasionally my father would help me escape, saying he did not think me quite well enough to go; did he not detect an oncoming cold?

At school I wore a scholar's long gown and mortarboard processing into chapel along the beautiful stone cloisters beside Liddell, soon to be killed in the war. We sang "Lord dismiss us". . at the last service each term. It was also the title of an amusing paperback about St. Columba's by Michael Campbell, second son of Lord Glenavy, about his days there which were also mine. The masters and some boys were thinly disguised. I found it highly entertaining whereas George White thought is scurrilous, I am not sure why.

Michael Campbell I met again when we were both working in the London Office of "The Irish Times", he reviewing art. It was he, too, who advised Dirk Bogarde to consider Thomas Mann's novella "Death in Venice" for a film; Visconti's famous production of it much later became my favourite film by far.

Once when I was 17 the Warden stood watching me playing tennis in my ambidextrous manner, with the tall, gaunt figure of Eamonn de Valera beside him. I doubt he noticed that the school tennis captain was playing with a very inferior racquet and worn balls. His "Irish Free State" had done little for the parents of its early member so isolated by circumstances. Anyhow I was now playing as a citizen of the newly created Republic of Ireland.

Towards the end of my last term the warden asked if any boys about to leave would like to become cadets with the Irish army during the holidays; I did not hesitate to refuse that challenge, even with its masculine overtones.

But two years earlier when he mentioned that Oxford Union scholarships were being offered for a year's education in America, I adventurously applied, with my parents' generous approval, as always. However, just before the time to go Sowby told my father that my education would suffer since the American standard for 16-year-olds was inferior – there would have been no Billy there anyhow.

My holidays were invariably spent at Thornfields, not being able to afford, or wish, to go elsewhere. I remember so clearly my last night there: I looked down the dormitory where all the boys were settling down for sleep and turned out the lights, thinking how much I would miss their company in future. A significant chapter was thereby closed.

Chapter five

Living in London

After my stay at St. Columba's I studied experimental science, including physics, chemistry and advanced mathematics at Dublin University for two years from October 1940, as well as music since in those days one could take extra subjects free. What a relief to go from a difficult lecture in organic chemistry to one on music given by Dr.Hewson, and attended only by two girls bored by the subject, who were merely studying it as part of some general degree. But admittance to Trinity also required passing in logic and latin, two particularly vile subjects. Latin I knew fairly well, yet scarcely a word of it can I recall today – how easily one forgets the unwanted.

At the end of my first term, sharing a flat at no. 27 with Hugh Massy from Rathkeale, also musical and studying science, I was awarded a ten pound science prize and immediately spent it on a music encyclopaedia. A radio I bought with an eighth share of a £100 crossword competition. Hugh and I would sometimes hear the first act of an opera relayed from the Gaiety Theatre and gate-crash the last two. Once we checked a tenor's doubtful high C by striking a tuning fork on a nearby seat. Another time he threw down a bouquet of Madam Butterfly roses to Joan Hammond, the famous Australian singer, having so enjoyed her performance in it.

But those were emotionally barren years, a vacuum after St. Columba's; almost the sole incident I recall took place near Ringsend in a summer meadow – almost like "an encounter" in James Joyce's "Dubliners". I was naïve enough to suggest to the friend that we meet again next year, same day, same month. Ever the optimist, I went along, but naturally he did not. How much more important a gay society, such as they have today, would have been, rather than the Historical Society, which I joined for its reading-room facilities.

At times we searched for 78rpm recordings in second-hand shops on the quays; Beethoven's late quartet op.127, Strauss's "Death and Transfiguration", and act one of Wagner's "Die Walküre" were our chief finds. The previous owner of the latter, an elderly lady, came to see who could possibly want to buy it, and told us about her many visits to Wagner festivals at Bayreuth to my delight.

Professor Ditchburn lectured us in physics, and one day in 1942, asked if anyone wished to volunteer for work as technical assistants at the Admiralty Research Laboratory, at Teddington, on the outskirts of London. By then I was finding the science course difficult, especially advanced mathematics, which hinged on continuity and never missing a lecture. So the thought of living in London appealed greatly, since it would give me access to music. I applied with my parents' support, as always, yet waited six months for a reply and only left in October.

Before setting off I heard Vaughan Williams' "London Symphony" and read a book with the same title, and knew I only required from blacked-out London one key item, a tall, dark-haired boyfriend. Strangely enough I thought I would meet him on Waterloo Bridge. On arrival, however, I found that music was not as readily available as I had imagined. I would open the "Daily Telegraph" hurriedly on a Saturday, and find only about four concerts listed, some perhaps out at Wimbledon or Golders Green. But at least the admission charges were usually low.

My digs down the road from the laboratory where I worked for about £23 a month were all right. Dr. Tunstead, head of my department, a stout chap about 30, had suggested I share the house owned by a Mrs. Glendinning, whose chief notoriety was her friendship with Nöel Coward's mother. Tunstead seemed to have no close friends of either sex and, on reflection, told me too many gay-related tales. Also I heard that when it was rumoured I was gay at the laboratory, he had hotly denied it; the rumour may well have stemmed from the fact I was keeping a photo of George prominent on my desk.

I would cycle the ten miles up to London on weekend afternoons to concerts, and at night go up by train through the blackout, returning to a cold supper left by my landlady. My first Saturday was typical; I went to the Wigmore Hall in the afternoon to hear the 80-year-old pianist Frederick Lamond, a pupil of Liszt, playing

Beethoven sonatas, and in the evening to Sadler's Wells Opera for Verdi's "Rigoletto".

After about a year – my aunt Esmée warned me not to go up during full moons when air raids were at their worst – I met Bertie Wilson at Sadler's Wells during a performance of "Swan Lake" with the young Margot Fonteyn already a prima ballerina. He was about 45, rather ugly with pouting lips, reasonably musical, and soon became very attached to me without encouragement. He began inviting me up for special performances after which I would promptly catch the train back to Teddington.

From September 1943, however, he invited me to use his small flat, so small in fact it had no bathroom and I had to use public baths at times, at World's End at the bottom of King's Road, Chelsea, which he only occupied at weekends since he was looking after an aged relative in the country during the week. There was an adequate dining-room, but only one bedroom, so Bertie would sleep in the sitting room at weekends. He wanted me to wear green shirts, which he bought, and thought I looked like Rupert Brooke – some hope – and wanted to wash my hair, which I generously allowed. I paid a pound a week nominal rent, and there it ended. I revealed nothing, and he made no further demands, except by implication leaving Wilde's "The Picture of Dorian Gray" as my bedside reading.

Perhaps I was unfair to accept the offer. His friends, who were mostly obvious gays, naturally imagined no such curious status quo. Once we hid in the basement flat of two celebrated lesbians during a particularly fierce air raid that demolished much of World's End in a single night. Indeed next morning I hardly recognised my route to Teddington through the awful rubble, so devastated was the scene. But perhaps, as often, I met halfway a young lad from the same department and cycled on, my arm around his shoulder whenever traffic permitted.

Very occasionally I went to bars in Soho with casual musical friends, one of whom lent me a first edition 1922 numbered copy of "Ulysses", little knowing its value. Nor did I, and five years later gave it away to a young hairdresser I hardly knew – and certainly not in the biblical sense – who was off to Australia. Not a bad tip!

On one such trip to Soho I nearly met my death when the bar was bombed, and part of the ceiling collapsed around me. I nipped down Leicester Square underground and stood shaking among the myriad people sleeping on mattresses laid along the platform until the 'All clear' siren went. It was on another occasion in Soho that I met Commander Foote, a wry name, who only endeavoured to command by taking me to tea at the Ritz, so totally unknown, as yet. More amusingly I remember a sailor putting his hand deep down into my pocket . . . only to dash away with a few loose coins.

That first summer I cycled up to the Royal Albert Hall for 49 of the 52 Promenade concerts such was my somewhat unselective thirst for music. I saw Sir Henry Wood conduct his last two concerts, and Dame Myra Hess playing on regardless of bombs crashing down in the distance. What if the roof of that giant building collapsed? A season ticket cost £7, for which you could stand right behind the conductor.

One evening I was rushing down the stairs to the favoured spot – it could be important what guy you stood next to especially for emotional music – when a test-tube of ammonia burst in my pocket. Why I had it there I cannot imagine, but it created a sensation amid the nearby Prommers. Three proms I missed only because I had to fire-watch at the laboratory. Rachmaninov died on one of the nights. What an odd thing to suddenly recall, but when you delve for memoirs much dross can arise unsummoned.

I had planned to go to a recital given by the Chiswick gramophone society on Sunday February 13th 1944. Why I changed my mind I know not, but it became by far the most important day of my life. I went instead for a walk to speakers' corner at Marble Arch, at the fairly respectable time of seven o'clock. By very dim lighting as was then permitted, one could see groups, chiefly male, standing around orators on their traditional soap-boxes, talking on any subject, being relentlessly heckled. I know exactly where I stood, and how far away George was listening to another group. It was not on Waterloo Bridge as I had anticipated, but there was my desired perfection.

We never decided who braved the intervening distance; it matters not. But as we walked to the bus to Chelsea I said to myself: "Here he is. Life would indeed be perfect if he were mine!" That moment, so cherished in my heart, is as clear now as more than 56 years ago. Before he died after our 42 superb years together – without ten clouded days, I reckon – he said: "Gerard, I have forgotten nothing you ever said to me, or anything we did together." I would not betray him now by going into details of our first night at 148 Elm Park Mansions, but just recall him also often saying: "This is exactly as it was the night we met . . ." I here apply a memoir writer's prerogative to retain one flimsy veil.

He revealed it was the first night he had ever stayed away from home; I was 22, and he was 24, the only older person to enter my affections. Our next meeting was a week later. It seemed endless; what if he did not turn up at our Hammersmith assignation? But he did, and we went so happily together to see his widowed mother Ede, whom he adored, living nearby in Brook Green. She had been in service many years, and had looked after her husband under great stress, since he was gassed in the first war, and only died in the second a year before I met my George.

He was an engineer at Sperry's Gyroscope company on the great West Road, and had worked there since he began as a grinder when about 16 years old. I still have the gold watch he was given for 15 years service, but more importantly the little perspex lighter he made me once on night-work soon after we met. He was not musical, and had once gone to "The Magic Flute" with his pal Terry, whose father dealt in paving stones, thinking it was a play. I met Terry, his straight friend for a year or two, and I last saw Billy briefly the week before I met George.

We had both been very solitary and self-sufficient to a degree; he was slightly tone-deaf, but over the years came to like Verdi, Richard Strauss and Mozart, but not Wagner except "The Flying Dutchman". His flat was small so I could not live with him and his mother, though we met on every possible occasion, when he was not working overtime, or on night duty. His was a reserved wartime occupation and they had refused his request to leave to join the navy; how terribly seasick he would have been. His mother, or he, cooked wonderful meals for us, and soon treated me exactly like a second son.

Without a conscious decision, our money quickly became jointly owner. I had very little and he often paid my way even, probably, for that first meal of mushrooms-on-toast opposite Charing Cross Station. I wonder whether the café is still there? He greatly like window-shopping, but I found it dull with no money to spend. Antiques fascinated him, especially in a shop at the end of his road that bought crystal lustres and assembled chandeliers. He wanted to buy a couple, but I stupidly did not like them.

We very seldom drank, knowing we could not afford it, and never sought the company of others. To that absence of drink in our early years I attribute my current well being. We would have a small amount at Christmas, some of which would likely remain until the next festive occasion. But what terrible digs I endured to live within a mile or so of his home after Bertie Wilson left me a note asking me to quit when he noticed I was bringing George there suspiciously often. Well, he had left "The Picture of Dorian Gray" by my bedside, and here was George who so closely resembled Hurd Hatfield then playing the part of Dorian in the film, on general release nearby. (By an amazing chance we met him thirty years later, retired to Co. Limerick, at a cocktail party. Our hostess introduced us to an ageing dapper gentleman sitting in the corner, showing some signs of wear and tear since he, alas, had no picture in the attic to receive it. She did say he usually kept a file of stills from the film at hand, in lieu.)

At first there was a room in a Chelsea flat which I shared with a young lad I had met at the Proms, who had however a very cloying nature, who George knew presented no threat whatsoever. Occasionally we had to raise our beds up against the window to protect us from flying glass in case a buzz bomb exploded nearby. We had seen many fly over, their engines suddenly cutting out to let them crash disastrously below. This happened near the end of the war.

Next I stayed some years in a horrid room at Mrs.

Gainsborough's house near Turnham Green. She was always trying different pretexts to bed me, and invariably asking me to fetch her gin immediately after I had paid my rent. Another woman whose name I thankfully forget had a fat gay son in the navy who when on leave would come into my room ostensibly to read me poetry. A variation was the night he woke me up calling out gleefully: "Peter, here are two cadets, one each!" I quickly refused his generous offer, thinking of my George. (Peter, my second name, I used all my life in England in preference to my first. George changed over easily when we came back to Ireland halfway through our lives.)

Finally I found Mrs. Reed's nice little house also near Turnham Green. Her husband, a lorry driver, I met by chance in a café nearby; she was a kindly stout woman, never grasping, always helpful, and I stayed with her several years. Accommodating she was too. Towards the end of my stay she let a room to Denis Tuggey, aged 20. He worked in a grocer's shop up the road, and owned a large dilapidated car, which he could no-way afford to run. I had bought my first TV, for £12 from a card in a shop window and Tuggey would sometimes come in to watch a film. One evening it showed African natives nude, but did not lower the camera sufficiently; he complained, and we laughed at our desire to see more detail - and so to bed.

Alas, Tuggey wanted money for the car, so one day stole a front and back cheque from my book. He filled in made-up names and tried to cash one for £140 at my bank. His effort failed but apparently he would have been paid out at once up to £100. I was contacted as to whether I had lost my book, and had to identify him at work; detectives told me they had to proceed against him even though I did not wish to take action. I told him if he tried describing our romps I would merely deny them; much hurt, he replied he would never renege so on my friendship. He was later let off as "more a fool than a rogue", after a few hours cooling-off in a cell.

Episodes such as this I related in detail to George. We kept no secrets from each other, after the first year or two, knowing that any straying when apart was purely physical, and could in no-way damage our undying love. Had we not prayed together at St. Paul's, on impulse, that it would last until death divided us, and so it was to be.

Soon after arriving in London while working at the laboratory chiefly on optics, such as night vision for which I once ate almost nothing but raw carrots for a week – it improved my night vision slightly – and the blooming of binocular lenses, and at shore establishments, usually taken there by Dr. Tunstead as his assistant, I bought my first motorbike, a monstrous Calthorpe 500 cc for £35. Needless to say it left much to be desired; I never saw another of that odd make, and fell off it several times before eventually taming it. (My father had a 1917 Rudge motorbike.)

Later however George and I made several pleasant weekend excursions on the monster. Idyllic days in the New Forest at Lyndhurst, or Rottingdean. We also went out to Esher at blackberry time, and there deep in the woods would strip off, oddly enough, while gathering them for jam. Luckily no one ever found us, so remote then were parts of Esher.

I needed leave of absence often to come back and see my parents since my father was frequently ill from amoebic dysentery which ultimately killed him in 1952 after he was bedridden for two years. Meanwhile a servant girl assisted my mother, in a house without electricity, but good though she was with him, she robbed my mother continuously. When I pointed this out – good items mysteriously disappeared from every unused room – my mother asked me to say nothing in case she would leave. A horrid blackmailer, in fact.

Eventually I decided to take the dreaded motorbike, which I used once to come back to Ireland, only to find it not loaded aboard at Fishguard, to a knacker's yard, and obtained £15 for it. A secondhand Lambretta scooter bought one November from a guy at Shannon was its successor. He listed the number of times he had nearly been killed on it, as he parted with it gladly for £50. Yet I sold it for £55 three years later with 25,000 miles added. But I disliked using it in Ireland on account of straying livestock, and potholes that neatly fitted scooter wheels. Its successor was a new blue one that took me safely on many journeys from London and to Covent Garden in the thickest traffic in a trice.

Soon after I met George he introduced me to a colleague of his, Freddy Rogers, a delightful guy who worked at his company's office as a draughtsman, and would come down to him on the shop-floor most days in the lunch-hour bringing books, perfume, and other tokens of affection. The first time George sent him to the Cambridge Theatre to join me at an opera, he wore a very fetching pale-blue corduroy jacket.

So began a very long and valued friendship, enduring to this day, and including all his family. (It was to him I turned soon after George's death, for comfort, driving my new Rover car much too soon amid motorway traffic, being so very shaken at the time. Once he came to Glyndebourne Opera in my mini-car, and very many times I enjoyed greatly his company at operas and concerts.) Occasionally in later years he turned up without notice at Thornfields when travelling for a medical company, but never spent the night. Yes, Freddy played a central role in our affections, and now the Staines magistrate always meets my return flights from abroad; but I cannot again enjoy London, alas, I am far too lonely there without my George.

A curious encounter I had at work at the laboratory in my lunchtime one winter, walking out in the snow in Bushey Park. There stood a beautiful blond German POW looking so forlorn and still. "Like a cigarette?" I ventured to ask. And so began an intense friendship with Helmut lasting more than two years. My lunches were neglected. I preferred to walk with him through the woods; occasionally he appeared out of the forest, like a deer seeking pasture, with another POW, but mostly we met alone. We never made an appointment for the next time, but always sought each other out.

He was later moved with his work-gang in 1947 to do gardening at Hampton Court, and my last memory is of him pushing a mower up a steep bank in those august gardens. Once he did come to my digs for tea – that was all. A few times I took a spare jacket, as his had an identifying large star on the back, and drove him down to Littlehampton far beyond his permitted ten-mile journey. George knew about him, naturally, but it so happened they never met. Occasionally we would hear from him at Christmas, but it was not until about six years ago that I finally saw him again at his lovely home between Aberdeen and Inverness with his wife Helen, who have recently visited me in Ireland for the first time, to celebrate his 70th birthday here. Oddly enough, he had never guessed I was gay, but they both accepted the fact perfectly, as no error in the makeup of a friend.

Several of our happiest weekends George and I spent at the

White Horse at Rottingdean, along the undercliff walk from Brighton, once on the princely sum of £10 given to us by my aunt Esmée for the purpose. He liked to see storms coming in from the sea, and to watch the movement of the waves, as did I. The only thing he did not like was being pursued by my camera. "Oh, you have enough photos of me by now", he would say so untruly, especially since his tall handsome figure was so very photogenic.

Naturally I found my one-room digs very cramped after Thornfields, or even my more spacious rooms in Trinity, but endured them to live near him, and earn a little money. Wealth, as such, I never sought, knowing it did not necessarily bring happiness. (I was considerably stung when the income tax people, doubting anyone could live on so little, wrote to say they had information that I was not disclosing all. I defied them to tell me if so, and that quickly ended the correspondence.)

As often as possible I would escape to Kew Gardens, never far away, there to enjoy the changing seasons, and space to ramble near the Thames, and admire the floral displays and hot-houses. Music also became escapism, with at least three concerts, operas or ballets weekly, or more if George was away working. I taught him to play bridge early in our relationship, and he soon liked it greatly and became a very good player.

For many years we had a men's four with Peter Burton whom I had met at the Wigmore Hall concerts during the war, his erstwhile lover Denzyl Ede, and Ray Thomsen sometimes, subsequently my closest friend in Sydney. Very occasionally we had lady opponents notably a lady conjuror – whom we debarred from using sleight of hand – and more interestingly Dora Brock, once a friend of Bosie, Lord Alfred Douglas. In Ireland we later played the game often with my sister and her husband Fred, and others; but now I like it less without George supplying knee-contact in the dull moments.

We both liked walking in the splendid royal parks and watching films. When I first met him we went very often to the cinema on which he was keen and knowledgeable. All our life we never once disputed which films or television we would watch; our tastes were exactly the same. That two solitary personalities could dovetail so perfectly was strange indeed.

When we first met I dressed very badly, partly from lack of funds but also because I took no pleasure in my appearance, and never considered myself in the least good-looking. I was wearing corduroys when we met, and he had handmade shirts bought in Piccadilly for 12/6 each. He had a wonderful colour sense, and admitted as an only child he had chosen his mother's hats from a very early age. Later at Thornfields I gladly deferred to his colour judgement – a lady called once, a colour consultant from Sandersons' wallpapers, and complimented him greatly on his choice.

His hands were always immaculate, remarkably so for an engineer, yet I never noticed him attending to them in any way. We used to meet at entrance five at Piccadilly Underground. Once standing there expectantly, I saw a stranger pass and noticing my smile when I saw George's distant figure, he remarked sadly "I wish that smile was for me."

In 1953 a year after my father's death, my mother moved to a small new bungalow at my sister's place twenty miles away, which she never liked after Thornfields which she had loved for more than 40 years. After ten lonely years there, without even television, she went down to the river, poor dear, leaving us a tender note. I fully understood her most tragic decision.

It was then very difficult to find tenants for the rambling overgrown visual ruin, while I remained in London. Ultimately in 1963 the place was so bad, and I was receiving only about £5 a week rent, from which I paid the rates, that I had to instruct an auctioneer to try and sell it with its twenty acres, mostly woodlands and scrub. About three months later the firm wrote saying the best offer was only £3,000. If they had said £13,000 I probably would have accepted reluctantly, knowing it was for demolition. No one could attempt, or afford to restore the mansion with more than 23 rooms.

So came about our hardest decision in our early forties, whether to move from London to save an otherwise extensive potential loss. One thing was certain, if we did move, we were going to buy a boxer dog, red-and-white, just like the one we always admired at George's butcher's shop. He was always so very considerate to all animals and the elderly.

When we did eventually decide to take on the huge operation, his manager told him he would employ him again gladly if the project failed, and offered him higher pay if he stayed on. "If I was not worth it while a service engineer never claiming excessive expenses I'm not worth it now", George rightly retorted.

I left the Admiralty Research Laboratory in 1948, disliking the work intensely, and found a job instead at the Post Office Savings Bank at Kew as a clerk, filing cards and such, which left my mind free to think about music – and George. Also I found I could obtain compassionate leave there more easily to return to Ireland to see my parents when necessary. Some of the women there made unpleasant remarks naturally when they eventually decided I was gay.

I enjoyed writing on music for "The London Letter" of "The Irish Times" from 1948 until 1964, on account of the free access it gave me to operas, concerts and ballet in London and abroad. But the money it brought scarcely paid my fares, and never once did they pay any expenses, merely allowing me to write for additional papers as well at times, such as the Toronto "Globe and Mail", "The Birmingham Post", and ultimately a monthly page in "Musical Opinion". I received five shillings for my first review.

Anyhow thereby I saw more than 200 different operas and some, such as Mozart's "Cosi Fan Tutte", my favourite if I had to choose one, more than 100 times on stage. As my mother rightly observed: "At least you will have music in your old age!" I always chose what I reviewed, reckoning I was not paid enough to hear music I did not like, or was not interested in for some extraneous reason. Never once did I suffer the indignity of having my copy edited; in any case it would have been very difficult to do so when I had to write so very concisely to fit a worthwhile review into about 300 words.

George first came to Thornfields as soon as the war ended and it was possible for him to do so, in 1947. Naturally my parents at once adored him. "Of course I love George because he loves you", my mother remarked in sweet simplicity, and my father asked him to look after me always. This first encounter with the very broken-down old place, lit by oil lamps and candles, and heated slightly by wood and turf might well have put off a lesser person from agreeing to its salvation in 1964. The decision as to whether to take the plunge he left to me out of deepest love, saying he would always support me completely wherever we lived.

Naturally I took him at once to all my favourite places. We explored the West Coast, and Kerry in particular, as well as the famous wild-flower Burren area, when we eventually settled back in

Ireland. Seafood we always sought, and all I can recall finding at the time were smoked mackerel at a pound each down near Dingle.

He came fishing with me, too, for small brown trout, both in lakes, enjoying the "evening rise", and in small rivers behind Thornfields. There we used to throw down our rods and roll in the grass, after looking for mushrooms, if in season. George always maintained that trout rose better if there was something worth seeing!

Before closing on my years in London I must mention my long friendship with Mrs. Kenyon. She was the matriarch of the chief London undertakers J.H. Kenyon, who had their premises, and her home in lower Church Street, Kensington. She had a box in the grand tier at the nearby Albert Hall, in an excellent side position, not too far away from the orchestra, and often gave me seats for concerts. She and her daughter June were very musical; the only drawback was the fact that June fancied me, without encouragement. Once I foolishly accepted a week's holiday at their nice home at Shanklin on the Isle of Wight. I drove down with her merchant navy brother, he on an ex-police Triumph and I on my old Calthorpe straining to keep up with his much better machine.

The weather was fine, but alas not the situation, with poor June making eyes at me while I sunbathed, and seeking secluded walks. The problem resolved itself, however, when on my return to London she almost at once announced her engagement to an insurance broker I had never even heard of.

I went to her wedding at which she chose, to my surprise, part of the Brahms' "German Requiem" composed for those who mourn. I still often called to tea with her mother; as my father once aptly remarked: "Gerry, at least you like ladies when they're over sixty!"

Naturally I found wartime London vastly different from the quiet of the west of Ireland. "Sir, do you realise you are ordering meat on a Friday?" I might be asked in Limerick. The general priorities still seemed church, self and state, reversed at a blow in London, with church a very bad third.

I always considered myself strictly neutral at heart, and had greatly admired de Valera's neutrality speech in April, 1941, in which he had said it was by the grace of God that Ireland was so, and it would be defended by force. I could not join British jingoism, gloating when German planes were shot down.

Anyhow not long after my arrival I found an unexpected ally in the inscription on Nurse Cavell's statue near the National Portrait Gallery: "Patriotism is not enough, I must have no bitterness or hatred for anyone". (She was executed in 1915, aged 50, for having helped more than 200 wounded soldiers to escape, and was later re-buried after a service in Westminster Abbey in 1919.) Also I sometimes found the British people in wartime, "too unhappy to be kind", to quote words by A.E. Housman, gay classical scholar and poet.

Chapter six

With George on the Continent

Usually George only had three weeks' holiday so we had to plan it very carefully being sure to leave him a day or two to recover before resuming his hectic work as a service engineer. Since I had much more free time, he let me make the arrangements, knowing I would plan the trip around our mutual interest in music. In this way our first continental holiday together was the ideal 'Paris in the spring', and as an exception we were to meet there briefly a colonel in the exiled Polish army, whom we only knew as "Mr. Pic". George had known a young friend of his in London.

We travelled by boat and train, and stayed opposite the Gare du Nord at the inexpensive "Hotel de Londres et New York", and conserved our very limited resources by eating frequently at the station off French bread and ham, washed down with drinkable vin ordinaire. It was 1948, and there were still signs of the German occupation especially in less frequented areas. Naturally we fell into the usual tourist pitfalls such as ordering "beer" on the Châmps Elysées and being confronted with the most expensive brand from some distant land. My schoolboy French helped slightly, but George spoke none.

How thrilling it was to walk those famous boulevards, with the trees in flower, where in later years I would bravely nip in and out of the hectic traffic on my scooter alone. How George liked the elegant window displays – we did not have much reason to go inside, except at "Printemps" which had its own wonderfully perfumed air – could it still, I wonder, these fifty years later.

Posters of the Opéra and Opéra Comique halted us several times, and we were lucky with the works on offer. One Saturday we had the interesting experience of hearing Gounod's "Faust" in the afternoon, and the much finer Berlioz "Damnation of Faust" the same evening – but not without being short-changed by a ticket-tout.

Wagner's "La Valkyrie" was also on offer at the fine Garnier Opéra, but we were unable to obtain seats together, and George was placed deep inside a narrow box whence he could see but little. At the end when the god Wotan surrounded his daughter Brünnhilde with fire, the company overdid the smoke effects, and George awoke, he admitted, thinking the theatre was on fire, rushed out, and tumbled down part of the Grand Escalier in alarm. The lazy chorus sang in French with the soloists declaiming German, a practise that remained there for several years.

The following day we went to the museum behind the Opéra and asked to see some mementoes of their greatest composer, in my opinion, Hector Berlioz. But evidently such he was not to the curator who had to delve through piles of souvenirs of Massenet and Gounod before he finally unearthed a small bronze of my hero. Afterwards we lunched, suitable enough, at the Paris Conservatoire, unchallenged, off tin plates to George"s disgust, where came alive the wonderfully evocative pages in Berlioz' brilliant memoirs, probably the finest musical autobiography of the 19th century, in which he related with gusto his many battles with their director, Cherubini.

Naturally we toured the sights such as the white pinnacled Sâcre Coeur, and Nôtre Dame Cathedral. But we visited the Louvre on an exceptionally hot day, and soon acknowledged our unfortunate ignorance concerning the works on display and left to relax elsewhere. (I regretted in later life how seldom I had visited museums while waiting for music at night.)

Soon it was Muguet Day, May 1st, when the French give sprigs of lily-of-the-valley, this beautiful tinkling flower, to their beloved. Naturally we did so, con amore, and walked along blissfully happy; the fact we could not afford to try the French cuisine did not worry us in the least.

That evening it was Weber's "Oberon" at the Opéra, and in the second act at the scene of Rezia's famous aria "Ocean thou mighty monster", the décor was green and white, and down showered the lovely Muguet perfume. The Paris Opéra had subvention far exceeding that of Covent Garden at the time, and could well afford such luxury.

Our first destination on the Metro was to see France's most famous cemetery, Père la Chaise, and pay homage at the grave of Oscar Wilde with its imposing memorial by Epstein. Here ended the brilliant but tragic life of the great writer, after he had briefly lived in exile in France, remarking finally to a friend who called, while he looked at some particularly revolting wallpaper, "either that must go or I". When one considers especially the "De Profundis", here was "a man of sorrow, and acquainted with grief".

We did not study carefully the map of all the celebrities buried there, but many names were familiar to us. Once so famous as his "Salome", Sarah Bernhardt lies only a few Salomes from Oscar Wilde's tomb. But I wanted to see particularly the newly prepared grave for the great young French violinist Ginette Neveu whom I had heard only a few months earlier giving such a memorable account of the Sibelius concerto at the Albert Hall, before she was killed in an air disaster along with her brother, Jean. There she lies buried with honour between the graves of Chopin and Bellini, with a broken violin depicted across her resting-place.

When we later met "Mr. Pic" he introduced us to his favourite cocktail that remained in three layers in the glass, one being green chartreuse, I think; we were much intrigued, and warmed by it content. He was a genial guide, who took us briefly to some gay bars, which were, however, of only passing interest so entwined already were our hearts. What a surprise we had the next day when we saw his face central on the front page of "Ce Soir" as the Polish delegate to some communist so-called peace conference taking place there at the time. The harmless secret was out to our amusement.

We visited the Opéra Comique for about its 1,565th performance of Bizet's "Carmen", sung with such apparent disinterest one could have imagined that the performances had taken place consecutively. Furthermore our cheap seats showed us as much obstructing pillar as stage. For "Mignon" and "Hamlet" we chose our positions with more care.

I cannot now consider returning to Paris alone, even to see the new "Bastille Opéra", since I was far too happy there with George. Just as when people now ask me whether I do not miss the lovely things we sold from Thornfields at our auction the week before he died, I reply truthfully since he cannot now see them I do not want to do so alone.

A standard short holiday at Sitges was the only package tour we ever tried. It so happened I had met a young English trainee matador at Covent Garden – no, not at "Carmen" – and on hearing I was soon off to Spain he lent me books on the so-called art of bull-fighting. I read them carefully and planned to see two bullfights in Barcelona, much to George's surprise.

On the first evening however we were both utterly appalled by what we saw. The barbarity of the actions and the cheering was so nauseating to hear, and for all the wrong reasons, that we almost wept. Such events are now continued chiefly to assuage the blood lust of tourists, I gather, and we were ashamed to be numbered among them that evening, although one poor bull had had limited success wounding his opponent temporarily.

We stayed at the pleasantly named Arcadia Hotel, which we found almost completed, and our room had not been double-booked. George, who could never even paddle in warm waters lest his legs went numb, though he never had any heart problem, spent his siesta in the room whereas I would stupidly lie out in the harmful sunshine, though exercising some caution. There was a religious festival in progress, and one day we walked along the central street on a bed of flowers spread in honour of the statue of Our Lady, soon to pass by.

Miss Bravo, by name not ability, escorted our tour up to the Montserrat mountain monastery to see the statue of the Black Virgin, 'Our Lady of Montserrat', said to have been carved by St. Luke, much venerated there; otherwise we spent our time solely together.

George agreed to buy good sherry for our room, but insisted on correctly patronising the hotel bar also. There one evening he trumped the barman nicely when he asked for a French brandy, and having barely tasted it returned it declaring roundly "I asked for French brandy, but you have given me Spanish!" (He also knew a barman's dodge of smearing the rim of a glass with neat gin to make you believe you have been given a gin-and-tonic of exceptional ferocity.)

I cannot imagine where he had gathered such knowledge of bar technique; the only elaborate dinner he had ever told me about was when a group of grinders from Sperry's decided to use some wartime extra money on a good dinner at the Clarendon in Hammersmith Broadway. But this had been somewhat marred, he related, when on seeing crêpe suzette, duly flambé, one grinder called out loudly: "Jesus, flaming pancakes!" much to George's embarrassment.

Belgium remained unknown to us, though I bounced alone over its horrid cobbles several times on my scooter en route to Germany. There we once spent an idyllic holiday at Coblenz, partly for the wine festival, with a trip also up the Mosel to visit the remarkable Burg Eltz, on a high pinnacle, one of Germany's best preserved medieval castles. The musical content was an operetta festival of casual interest, ending inevitably with the tenor being thrown into the Rhine.

But alas one evening George unwisely drank beer after wine, and was hugely ill, cold as ice, all night much to my alarm; thus one learns more of life's many pitfalls. We also took the badly vibrating steamer up the Rhine to beyond St. Goar, passing the famous "Loreley" rock from which a maiden crossed in love once threw herself into the Rhine far below. Now her voice still lures fishermen to their death on dangerous rocks beneath its fast flowing current – unless they happen to be gay!

Munich became George's favourite city, and its summer heat was seldom too much for him. Who does not delight in walking where the Isar River rushes along by pleasant meadows still preserved from development I hope. How beautiful are the chimes of the twin-towered Frauenkirche, and merrily the ancient mechanical clock on the Town Hall façade marks the passing day. Nearby stands the relatively new pillar; about eight feet high inscribed with scenes from Richard Strauss's operas. (All 14 of these except his first "Guntram" deemed too Wagnerian even for Munich, I saw there through the years; "Daphne" was the last I attended. Strange, too, how much his music joins Wagner to Mozart, just as Munich joins Bayreuth to Salzburg geographically. It was Richard Strauss that rescued Mozart's "Cosi Fan Tutte", his favourite opera, from near oblivion in about 1885.)

We were never in Munich for the famous Oktoberfest, and a young Bamberg lawyer friend of ours adamantly refused to be seen drinking in the Hofbrauhaus – far too plebeian.

Some years George would join my musical merry-go-round there flying out from London. Our best such holiday was when we went south about twenty miles to Starnberg lake, after performances at the lovely Prinzregenten Theatre.

There we rented a small paddle-boat and after about an hour's exertion reached the far end of the lake, where we saw beside us amid the rushes, a small wooden cross inscribed in memory of King Ludwig II, at the place he was found drowned alongside the body of his warder psychiatrist Dr. Gudden. It was he who caused the King's imprisonment in 1886 declaring him subject to irreversible paranoia. It was while on an evening walk from Castle Berg where he had been held prisoner initially that the dreadful tragedy happened.

From our bedroom window at Füssen further south, a few days later we looked out directly at Neuschwanstein castle floating, it seemed, above the pines, a memorable sight. After visiting the old Hohenschwangau castle, the royal family residence where Ludwig and his young brother Otto, who later went insane, played in their youth, we took the winding road up to Neuschwanstein, just as did the posse of officials from Munich coming to arrest their king. They accused him of neglect of duties, among other things, while living in regal isolation surrounded by handsome courtiers, some of whom accompanied him on rides at night in his golden sleigh, still preserved in a Munich museum.

We passed through the gateway made with sandstone from Bayreuth – the king constructed his castles in honour of Wagner, believing them to be the counterpart of the great "Ring Cycle", architecture being frozen music as Goethe believed. We came soon to the magnificent singers' hall where concerts are still occasionally held, with frescos from Wagner's works, chiefly "Lohengrin" for a castle overlooking the Schwansee, core of the ancient legend.

Nearby we saw the turrets from which the king wished to throw himself when it seemed imprisonment was inevitable. He had also asked a close friend to obtain quickly poison according to Visconti's splendid four-hour film "Ludwig" that could detail exactly what happened, it was so relatively recent, Wagner had only been dead three years.

At first the king imprisoned the group in his new dungeons, until finally resistance proved impossible. When I first went there the gardener who found the king in the lake was still alive, and I happened to meet a lady whose father had been the surgeon who cut out the king's heart, buried separately in the Wittlesbach tradition. "I wish to remain an enigma to myself and to the world", the king once wrote, and it is still uncertain exactly how the drowning occurred.

We did not go as far as his Linderhof castle where a grotto has a swan-shaped skiff in which the king was wont to sail; there too, he entertained the young actor Kainz from Munich, who was ordered to give long solo performances, just as back in Munich in his early days the king, it is said, attended about 200 performances alone in various royal theatres.

The king's other great castle Herrenchiemsee, on an island in the Chiemsee, we visited for a concert by candlelight in the famous gallery of mirrors, longer than that of Versailles. "L'etat c'est moi!" was the motto Ludwig adopted from his admired French monarch. A string quartet played music by Mozart and Haydn, reflected endlessly, as befitted such grandeur. Earlier we had seen sketches the king made when only twelve years old of imaginary fairytale castles from his extraordinary imagination. But then we came abruptly to a brick wall where all the opulent blue-and-gold regal splendour ended suddenly. The king's huge personal extravagance was never, in fact, a liability on the state – which now anyhow gains so much from his projects. We heard also how royal gold watches were still occasionally being taken to Bavarian auction rooms by former lovers now grown old.

Our next destination was Garmisch, which we reached on a very hot day after about a three-hour bus journey in a single decker vehicle that the driver imagined expandable stopping continuously until it was just about double-loaded. Then after a very necessary rest in a wine cellar, we sought Richard Strauss's beautiful villa on the outskirts of the town, built in 1905 with money from his first great operatic success "Salome" based on Oscar Wilde's drama. (The composer first saw it in the French translation, apparently, and on being asked was it not a suitable subject for him too, he replied "I'm already working on it!")

The Strauss family was still living in the villa, headed by his son Franz, called after his grandfather who was first horn with the Munich State Orchestra and advised Wagner on the Siegfried horn calls. We found admission was only granted briefly at other times. Having come so far, I hoped to be able at least to take a photograph and ventured briefly onto the lawn, when up drove a large white car and out stepped the owner; we explained we had come out of homage, and apologised for our intrusion, whereat he kindly invited us to come and see his father's study where so many of my favourite scores were composed. (Even as a boy at Thornfields I had read about the première of his opera "The Silent Woman", and the first books I took out of Limerick library were "The Correspondence of Richard Strauss and Hugo Von Hofmannsthal" and "The Libretti of Wagner's "Ring Cycle".)

Around Strauss's study were several important paintings since the composer was a shrewd investor in art I was told by a friend of mine, Lady Mabel Dunn, who stayed with the family before the war. It was here Frau Strauss kept strict order as a dominant personality, daughter of a Bavarian general. Strauss met her first when he conducted "Tannhauser" at Bayreuth when only 29 – "How young you are, yet how well you conduct", Cosima Wagner had remarked. His future wife, Pauline de Ahne had sung Elisabeth.

While we were being shown around Strauss's home, I could hear within, his "Domestic Symphony" in which he described life at Garmisch in detail, even to the cries of his infant son, now our guide. Outside towered the Alps, including the Zugspitz, and other mountains that the composer liked to climb in his younger days, and illustrated so excitedly in his "Alpine symphony". In lavish rose beds I was tempted to look for a silver one such as Octavian bears so elegantly in his masterpiece "Der Rosenkavalier". Also somewhere in the garden Strauss once marked a grave to denote the demise of his first opera "Guntram", I was told.

Not long after this memorable visit to Strauss's lovely home we attended a performance of his autobiographical opera – the only one I imagine – "Intermezzo" and saw Franz in the stalls watching himself portrayed as the young son. It is an amusing domestic drama, portraying a jealous wife's mistake on hearing a well-known conductor, also initialled R.S. had made an assignation with an infamous Viennese courtesan. A game of skat, which Strauss liked so much, is seen, and the opera has a delightful stage entry when Baron Lumner, with whom the wife hopes to dally in revenge, comes swoosh onto the stage down a toboggan run. All is resolved, of course, and the opera, which has been staged at Glyndebourne, ends with the composer pouring out his true love for his bossy wife in some of his most endearing music.

One summer George joined me at the Salzburg festival for a few days, it was, strangely enough, a city he did not like especially. I showed him around, not forgetting the graves of Nannerl and Constanze Mozart, and some of its many very beautiful churches; but it was very hot, and our pension run by genial Frau Nussbaum – Mrs. Nuttree – was too far out for convenience. I only had single press seats there, and would meet him after the performances, some times at an ice-cream parlour for a cassatta, after he had been window-shopping, and perhaps refusing offers like when somebody in Munich vainly implored him to go for a stroll in the notorious English garden at dusk. Then we would have a glass or two of wine and retreat happily to bed.

During my previous Salzburg visits I often went by scooter for day trips to the lovely Salzkammergut lake region, sometimes to St. Gilgen to see my favourite Mozart statue depicting him aged about ten, playing his violin. But with George I decided instead to spend a few days at Gmünden on the Traunsee after the festival.

We went by train down to the lake on a spur off the main Salzburg-Vienna line, drawn by a rickety old engine, rolling stock still being scarce for minor lines, that George suggested might well have been last used by Franz Josef and uncleaned since then.

Instead of staying in the town centre, after a good look around, we decided to walk a kilometre or so along the left bank and seek a quiet pension for our stay. We were soon lucky finding "Haus Traugott" – "God's Sorrow" we ignored – which was run by a friendly Austrian lady and her two young daughters. Our meals were served beside a willow at the lakeshore, and our bedroom had a blue ceiling with golden stars – as once had the Sistine Chapel.

On our third day we walked back into town and saw a small yacht for hire; but neither of us had ever tried one of any description. I can swim moderately well, but George could not swim a stroke. The sun blazed down and there was not a ripple on the lake, so I decided to take one out alone, overlooking the fact no life jackets were provided, if there was wind enough.

Then I made a terrible decision, probably the worst of my life. I drew in, and said to George: "Come on, this is easy!" There was no sign by then of the owner to check the apparatus or advise us in any way. On we gently sailed admiring the lovely scenery, and chatting away as usual. We did not notice that the shore was becoming ever more distant and finally we were almost out of sight of anyone. There were very few other yachts around, and those that were noticed the storm approaching.

We, however, had seen nothing until suddenly the yacht was thrown mercilessly from left to right. It was as much as we could do to avoid the boom, and we did not even know what ropes were attached where. In our terror it did not occur to us to undo everything in sight to try and let down the sail. Over it tilted to the water's edge, this way and that; I realised if it capsized I would have

68

great difficulty holding up George who was much heavier than I. Soon I became resigned to our impending fate. At least we would go together; but what of our dear widowed mothers still both alive?

How long we were thus battered I cannot say, but ultimately I managed to point the wretched craft in the direction of the shore, not minding in the least if I wrecked it in the shallows, when the storm abated. We drew in near "Haus Traugott" by chance, and George stepped out into shallow water, greatly relieved, and I managed to take the yacht along near the shore and retrieve my deposit from the unconcerned owner. Since then I have considered inexperienced sailing stupid in the extreme when a lake can be admired much more agreeably from the safety of the shore. George suffered only bad sunburn, but our holiday was ruined since we both suffered delayed shock, and were ready to leave, rowed sedately across the corner of the lake to the town by the two young daughters of the house. In this way our joint life, and the second half of these memoirs, so very nearly foundered.

Our last and most enterprising continental trip took place in 1963, the year before we returned to Ireland to save Thornfields, and two years after my mother's death, when I bought my first car. George was glad to see me discard my last scooter; little could he have imagined me motor-cycling gleefully in northern Thailand 40 years later! We chose one of the first red mini-cars; the first time I filled it up I was told sourly: "That's only a small tin box, you'll certainly kill yourself in it." Not a very generous launch. Soon I took it to Amsterdam, nearer to London than Fishguard, for part of the Holland Festival in June, and George joined me there later.

He knew I went there sometimes to the famous DOK gay club, one of the first official retreats, but naturally I thought no more of it once he appeared. Equally he was much to shy to join me there, or at a nude beach; obviously we allowed some slight differences in character. The red mini was a rare sight then parked by the canals, and looked quite smart. I soon found it had such a low centre of gravity it was virtually impossible for it to skid. Once I even drove it alone from Bristol to London with scarcely another car in sight and snow packed high on either side, completely against AA advice, without the slightest skid, anxious to see George quickly.

Perhaps it was because he was slightly dyslexic, as I only found out in later life, that he was a bad map reader, but against that he was a perfect passenger never criticising my driving which he thought very good, unless in a dire emergency.

Off we set to drive to the Riviera for about a week, with adequate maps and enough cash for our modest needs. We never booked in advance, but when evening approached would sight a small village and turn off a kilometre or so and stop there in rustic quiet at 'Zum Post', or such, usually an ideal resting-place.

The roads were less congested then and we easily escaped the orbit of Amsterdam, which I knew well from previous visits. The mini seemed a very big improvement on my scooter especially in rain, and George would just assist me in the overtaking problem inherent in a right-hand drive vehicle. Fast continental cars looked in surprise at the capabilities of our tiny car, and one petrol attendant nearly added water to its petrol tank in ignorance of its layout.

We committed an offence on a southern German autobahn running out of petrol, anticipating it cheaper in Switzerland. It was up to me, the more mobile, to cross fields to a distant village and return proudly carrying a small amount in a watering can, duly returned. Next we went up the Swiss Alps in the little car, so very light to drive, and there encountered slight snow falls to vary the lovely scene. Then it was an enjoyable drive down to Lake Como where we spent some hours resting and absorbing its exceptional romantic beauty, having passed a 'William Tell' village en route.

Once into Italy we were rather annoyed to find we could only use their main roads on payment of a toll, and when we reached Milan we decided not to bother seeing "La Scala", where I have never been, and eventually found the road for Genoa only after encircling the city twice, or so it seemed. What an ugly place Genoa looked, or the small part of it we were forced to observe through lines of lorries and huge dirty containers, belching oil. We gladly gave it a wide berth and drove on.

Eventually we decided to spend a few days at Alassio on the Italian Riviera. I meanly insisted on booking into a pension directly on the seafront, whereas George would have preferred wisely something at least a little way inland. Anyhow when we found we had to pay to use the dirty beach, and everywhere were jostling noisy tourists, we agreed to flee to the highest point overlooking the city.

We set off early, and when confronted by a T-junction took the named route but it merely landed us in a small hotel car park, and the instruction had been painted on a wall, not on a twisted signpost. We tried again with the same result; so next time we took the only other option with success. (I told a tourist office of our dilemma, when happening to pass one, and to our amazement we found the error amended almost at once.)

High in the hills overlooking the beautiful coastline we lay down together at a fruit farm, oblivious of all, having a large quantity of their produce by our side. This was our somewhat unusual daily occupation while staying there, reflecting perfectly our total engrossing compatibility.

On our last night we happened to wake at about 4:00 am and George had the brilliant idea of leaving forthwith; we paid the night porter and fled so as to have the 'grand corniche' drive to ourselves.

We came to Cannes and Nice approaching from elevated roads and stopped at times to rejoice in the spectacle of the sea mists dispersing at dawn. We joked about gays, overt and covert, now awakening with their spoils of the previous evening in disarray, in these two playgrounds of the rich. I expect we agreed how much more pleasant it would be to awaken "Under Milk Wood", even with no infusion of Welsh blood. (We had both heard its radio première, and seen its first stage presentation at the New Theatre, and Dylan Thomas's inspired work was often in our minds.)

When we then passed through Bordighera I told George how my mother when 23 years old had stayed there as a companion to a wealthy American lady from Co. Limerick, for a month or so. We found photos in ancient panorama of them dressed in Edwardian clothes, setting off on mules for a day out in the hills. But there had been a more amusing episode, apparently, when her wealthy patron's large bag of sovereigns slipped from her grasp at the head

71

of the stairway and Midas-like a shower of gold had fallen from on high. The staff rushed wildly to return but a fraction of the Nibelung's hoard.

In this leisurely way we reached Monte Carlo in good time for breakfast, which we enjoyed in a small café having ample fare for about £5, tax free I presume, before spending the next two hours touring the small principality. Naturally I wanted to drive part of the Grand Prix course, since we both often enjoyed it on television, though knowing little of its technicalities. Our sedate mini-lap would not have qualified, alas but what fun it was, completed before gendarmes appeared to control another summer's day. Later we passed the casino where the famous, including many leading tennis players, try their fortune with money they save by living in this tax-haven, or saying they do so. The Grimaldi Palace we admired, too, before leaving Monte Carlo claiming a record for the cheapest visit yet made there by two people.

We then began our drive back over the French Alps, and once had to stop while hailstones the size of marbles danced wildly off our windscreen to our alarm. During the ensuing downpour we drove on carefully, and were suddenly confronted by a lady in a white blouse standing in the centre of the road waving her arms excitedly imploring us to slow down. Naturally we did so and were possibly saved from running into a bad accident just around the next corner, which we passed slowly, checking whether assistance was required.

After an exceptionally long but wonderful day during which I had driven about 400 miles, we decided to mark the occasion in central France by at last lashing out on an evening of good French cuisine – chosen by my adviser as our elderly solicitor, Catherine Tynan, invariably called him and was indeed his due.

Chapter seven

Great Musical Occasions

"If music be the food of love, play on,
Give me excess of it, that surfeiting,
The appetite may sicken and so die . ."

The opening of "Twelfth Night" which was the only Shakespeare play I studied at school, since my mind was so singularly focused on music. So in this chapter I look at some of the great musical events I attended before I left London in 1964. My forty-two wonderful years with George were almost exactly divided between London and Ireland.

Three years after I first reviewed music for "The Irish Times" from London I planned a visit to the 1951 reopening of the great Wagner festivals at his own theatre at Bayreuth in northern Bavaria. Also I was to hear a Wagner performance in Munich en route, and afterwards attend the first of my eleven consecutive Salzburg festivals. Although performances had been given at Bayreuth up to 1941, with the German hierarchy in attendance including Hitler on many occasions, the reopening marked the renewal of the festivals begun in 1876 with the first complete performance of Wagner's great "Ring Cycle".

He chose Bayreuth for the theatre devoted exclusively to his works, after being hounded out of Munich – for which it was originally planned – partly on account of his affair with Cosima von Bülow, daughter of Franz Liszt, wife of the Munich court conductor, who even gave the première of Wagner's "Tristan" – greatest of his love music – precisely while his wife was giving birth to Wagner's daughter Isolde, named after the Irish princess. Dublin's Chapelizod retains the name. Wagner wrote the libretti for all his operas, and oddly enough wrote those for the "Ring" in reverse order over some 27 years, showing remarkable perseverance.

On my way to Bayreuth I stopped in Munich, a wonderful city to see for the first time with its swiftly flowing Isar River; it later became George's favourite city. There I heard "Tannhaüser" a great middle-period work in the Prince Regent Theatre also with a sunken orchestra pit. The famous Max Lorenz sang the lead with the aged

Robert Heger conducting. Next morning I took the train up to Bayreuth, very rickety with battered rolling-stock at the time, passing forests on the way to badly bombed Nüremberg where I just paid a quick courtesy call on the statue of Hans Sachs, the cobbler featured in the "Mastersingers of Nüremberg". Strangely enough it had survived the terrible devastation, as has Cologne Cathedral which I also saw standing alone in a city almost bombed to oblivion.

The train up to Bayreuth passed through valleys and by rocky prominences on which one almost expected to see Valkyrie maidens from the operas. The festival was given in "the silly little town in north Bavaria", as Bernard Shaw dubbed it, when he often attended the early festivals in his youth when one of the greatest music critics. Many people were in national Bavarian costume wearing lederhosen, seldom seen today alas, and had leisure to watch the international audience arrive. Over the theatre, still only a temporary structure since its acoustics are so perfect they never dared change them, flew one flag with Wagner's monogram in red.

After Wagner laid its foundation stone 80 years earlier, characteristically placing next to it a verse of his own – always the supreme egotist, but with justification – he went down to the Margrave's old opera house, built 200 years earlier and then having the largest stage in Germany, to conduct Beethoven's ninth symphony in tribute and hope, having always shown great interest in the work.

So it was chosen to reopen the 1951 festival. Just before 8 o'clock fanfares heralded the performance, and I went up to the gallery from which King Ludwig II of Bavaria "the last artist to sit upon a throne", as he has been correctly called, saw the first performances hidden from the other German rulers whom he despised. Yet it was he who made the completion of the "Ring" possible and the theatre itself, and certainly the composition of Wagner's final opera "Parsifal" by his continual support. When the king, aged 18, became Bavaria's gay monarch in 1864, he wrote immediately to Wagner then a political refugee in Switzerland "It is for you I wear my crown, tell me what your will is and I will obey". One of the greatest ever examples of royal patronage.

The original red-and-white curtains parted to reveal the huge orchestra drawn from all the great German orchestras, and the festival choir with reawakened bats flying overhead. Wilhelm Fürtwangler conducted magnificently with Schwarzkopf, Höngen, Hopf and Edelmann as soloists. Permission to reopen had only been given on condition that Wagner's daughter-in-law Winifred Wagner, who went before a de-nazification court on account of her very close friendship with Hitler, handed over the direction to her two sons, Wieland and Wolfgang, then in their early thirties. Oddly enough her husband Siegfried, Wagner's only son, died in 1930 the same year as his mother Cosima.

Winifred, who was English, had the difficult task of running the festival from 1930 until 1941. I met her and her sons during the festival; Wieland, the elder, had studied art during the war in Munich and was the only German excused military service as the heir to Bayreuth, but his brother Wolfgang was slightly wounded on the Russian front.

At a luncheon Winifred Wagner told me much about those years, including how she knew all eleven of Siegfried Wagner's operas – never staged today – before she met him, a strange courtship indeed! She also described helping the very aged Frau Cosima into the Wagner box, and calming her down if she noticed any slight variations from Wagner's very explicit stage instructions. Shaw had written there was a danger of Bayreuth becoming "a temple of dead tradition instead of an arena of live impulses". After attending the early performances of "Parsifal" he wrote: "this Parsifal is a wonderful experience, not a doubt of it", which I certainly endorsed the next evening. (Comparing Parsifal and Tristan, Shaw observed: "To admire Parsifal it is necessary to be a philosopher or a fanatic, but to admire Tristan it is only necessary to have had one serious love-affair".) To hear the prelude to either float out of total darkness, the sunken orchestra-pit allowing no light to emanate, is musical perfection, precious Bayreuth moments treasured to this day.

Now directed by Wolfgang Wagner, since his brother's early

death, I hear that very eccentric productions are now staged there, often horrifying the 'perfect Wagnerites' among whom I count myself having attended some forty performances there in the following 12 years. In 1963, the 150th anniversary of Wagner's birth, the city of Bayreuth sent me a gold medal for my reportage of the festivals, which pleased me greatly. The 'friends of Bayreuth' wear a gold ring in their lapels – but are not sworn to speak Irish!

Winifred showed me privately around the Wagner home, the Villa Wahnfried – 'free from care' – given by King Ludwig to Wagner, which was then Wieland's home. It was slightly bombed in the war, and Wagner lies buried at the bottom of the garden where his Cosima was reunited with him 47 years later though she had expressed, in her extensive diary, the wish to die in the selfsame hour as Richard. (I chanced one day to meet a young German who told me, he was another descendant of Liszt, whom he did not know was also buried at Bayreuth, so I quickly took him to see the grave outside the small church where Wagner and Cosima were ultimately married.)

When American troops reached Bayreuth at the end of the war, they looted the great theatre trotting round Bayreuth wearing various props. They also gave the theatre the final insult of staging "Madame Butterfly" there, and cabaret for the troops. It was partly on account of this outrage that the famous new productions, often staged on vast tilted saucers, with lighting taking the place of realism, resulted to reduce costs. Wagner's strict stage directions were frequently broken but to great imaginative effect.

The festival began with "Parsifal" the sacred stage-drama which Wagner originally hoped would only be staged at Bayreuth, not to be contaminated by general repertory, a very laudable idealistic idea, retained for about a decade. Hans Knappertsbusch was the conductor, whom I greatly admired, and the young Herbert von Karajan conducted "Mastersingers" that caused some extra nationalistic cheering with its 'German Art' emphasis, as was perhaps inevitable so soon after the war.

The new style had a great influence on opera production in Europe for the next two decades. After the preliminary night I was given a very good press seat for all performances, to my delight. Once Winifred Wagner changed it for a seat in the Wagner box for a performance of "Lohengrin", a thrilling occasion seated in the box as in Wagner's time, and with the theatre's superb acoustics – but was I perhaps in Göering's seat?

I could rarely afford to go to Wagner's favourite tavern "The Owl" after a performance. But once I did, seeing "The Meister's" favourite chair, having passed murals of scenes from his son's operas, and photos from the early Bayreuth productions. (The orchestra still in some cases plays from original parts. Singers cannot dry-up since the text is read softly throughout, a friend once told me who had been smuggled into the pit for a performance.)

It was a very amusing evening at "The Owl". A rich owner of a ball-bearing factory in the Rühr was there with a very gay entourage of young friends, and asked me to join their party. I was reminded of my young friends larking around in Berlin after my opera début when fifteen years old. Soon I was alerted by the attentions of a black youth who pleaded with me to take his master's big Mercedes and drive him through the forests forthwith; perhaps he had succumbed to Wagner's love music, or a little too much schnapps. Although he assured me I would not be disappointed, prudence forbade the adventure.

At Bayreuth I also met my German friend Günter – 37 years ago, as he often reminds me today. It was at another "Parsifal" evening, and he looked very smart and jovial chatting with other young Germans. There was also a remembered festive romp with an American GI named Garland O'Rear. Nowadays I hear it is virtually impossible to obtain tickets such is the demand; one man of 85 pleaded with the box-office not to reject his application for the eighth time in view of his age, and they relented. George came there one year for a week, but refused even to look inside the great theatre when I met him as usual after the performance, during which he might have enjoyed a nice meal instead, quite rightly. But to show him off was always satisfaction and delight – and more.

I often went there on my Lambretta scooter, which my Bayreuth friends christened "Grane" after Brünnhilde's horse. The wonderfully reliable machine – just as well it and I stayed fit, as I seldom had an extra £10 with me – I parked nonchalantly among the splendid cars atop Bayreuth's green-hill. Martha Mödl, Birgit Nilsson, Wolfgang Windgassen, Fischer-Dieskau and Hans Hotter were among my favourite singers there during those years.

Winifred Wagner had also told me when she engaged Richard Strauss to conduct there, she sometimes had to find opponents for him to play the German card game skat with, and indemnify them against the inevitable losses, since he was such an expert.

After Bayreuth I went down, as in future visits, to Salzburg, most beautiful of Austrian cities, where Italian and northern cultures combine so very gracefully. Richard Strauss and Von Hofmannsthal founded the festival in 1925. There I had the great excitement the next year of attending the first performance of Strauss's last opera "The Love of Danae", given posthumously, delayed by the war, Below the fortress heights lie so many fine churches as well as the cathedral in front of which the morality play "Everyman" is staged annually. At St. Peter's in particular I heard annually the lovely Mozart "Mass in C minor" where it was originally given to celebrate his marriage to Constanze who sang at its première. At other churches I often went to Sunday services to hear Haydn and Mozart masses in their correct setting. I usually stayed a week or ten days enjoying greatly my press facilities.

There the Rocky Riding School is an extraordinary wide stage for opera or drama, hewn out of the cliff face. "Don Giovanni" I often saw there under Fürtwangler with Schwarzkopf, Simoneau, Walter Berry and other great singers. At the Mozarteum academy there were frequent Mozart matinées, at one of which I heard one of his violin concertos written when he was 19, played on his own violin, and his birthplace in the Getreidegasse has an excellent museum.

By day I would swim, or go for drives on my scooter, once up to Berchtesgarden overlooking the Königsee, to see Hitler's "Eagle's Nest" fortress hideout – then occupied solely by a goat asleep inside. The ruins seemed eerie in the extreme. In Salzburg itself there was a nice sauna in a park for relaxation, where once when in Salzburg in January 1956 for the Mozart bi-centenary I had a snowball fight, only to see my opponent among the first violins of the Vienna Philharmonic, which plays all through the festival, the following night. A special occasion too was a reception in the Archbishop's Palace at which Mozart's serenades were played, to be talked through, in the foyer for which they were written.

On January 27th 1956, the bi-centenary of Mozart's birth I saw the Austrian government in attendance at a special performance of the "Coronation Mass" to mark the occasion. At night candles shimmered everywhere against the snow around the central Mozart statue, which his widow Constanze saw erected there just before her death in 1842 in a house overlooking the square.

In London I earlier went to the opening of the Royal Festival Hall which was built in 1951 as part of the Festival of Britain on the south Bank. Naturally the greatest care was taken to obtain acoustics of the highest quality; and to this end various adjustments were possible within the hall once the main structure was completed.

I went to a special tuning concert in which the London Philharmonic Orchestra played works such as the powerful "Mastersingers" overture, and pistol shots were fired while technicians measured the period of reverberation, as it is called. Various holes in the ceiling could be opened or closed until the precise required tone was achieved. An especially ingenious arrangement was the placing of holes under the seats so that upturned they absorbed the same as when occupied, so the quality did not depend on the size of the audience.

All that resulted in slightly dry, clear acoustics, as good as ever I encountered. On the actual opening May 5th, 1951, the Archbishop of Canterbury led the service of dedication. State trumpeters announced the arrival of the royal family, and King George VI unveiled a commemorative tablet. Choristers of the Chapels Royal were in attendance in scarlet and gold robes. Sir Adrian Boult, wearing academic robes, conducted the hymn "All people that on earth do dwell" followed by Sir Malcolm Sargent, who then conducted the "Hallelujah Chorus" during which the audience remained seated, to my surprise, breaking the tradition begun by George II that all should stand in its honour. Vaughan Williams' "Serenade to Music" and the jingoistic "Rule Britannia" completed the event.

The fine building became my frequent haunt in subsequent years, attending about every ten days when in London. One of my earliest visits was to see the very aged Toscanini conducting on his last visit to London, two Brahms symphonies; I had an excellent view of the famous man from a seat behind the orchestra for once. Other similar notables I encountered then included Elisabeth Schumann giving her last London recital, Cortot, Schnabel, and above all the great Norwegian soprano Kirsten Flagstad, probably the finest soprano I ever heard.

I base that on her performances, just after the war, as Isolde, despite placards outside Covent Garden declaring her husband a Nazi sympathiser. Her magnificent voice soared supremely in the great theatre when I repeated the tremendous experience, on subsequent occasions. (I had peeped into the theatre on my arrival in London in 1942 to see it packed with American GIs dancing with their molls, and fled.)

I heard her again, when 60 years old, giving her last Albert Hall recital including several Grieg songs, such as I once heard in his home at Bergen, and again when she gave the thrilling first performance of Richard Strauss's "Four Last Songs" conducted by Fürtwangler in May 1950. But stranger was the time when she sang in Purcell's "Dido" in a very small theatre casually constructed at the bottom of the garden of her friend the actor Bernard Miles, with Maggie Teyte. Flagstad's contract was unique; she was to be given two pints of stout a day, flowers, fruit and foliage, and be waited on by the children who were instructed to take every opportunity to make her laugh. It was sealed with a kiss.

The Royal Ballet I was visiting meanwhile, along with visits by the Kirov and Bolshoi companies once they were in action again. The Ballet Rambert and the Kurt Joos companies kept me busy, too.

It was when covering a performance by the royal ballet dancer Beriosova that I gave "The Irish Times" probably its best misprint ever. She danced an Ashton Ballet with all grey décor and wore a red rose corsage that contrasted beautifully . . . but not in my review, which read: "grey décor relieved only by the ballerina's red nose"!

In 1955 "The Irish Times" wrote to the Vienna State Opera asking if I might have a press seat for their long-awaited reopening on November 5th, also marking Austrian independence. To my delight they invited me to all six premières within the special festival. Since March 12th 1945, when it was utterly destroyed so near the end of the war, they had restored the magnificent opera house at a cost of more than three million pounds.

So on a sharp autumnal day only the red-and-white flag of free Austria flew aloft, opposite flags from thirty other nations including Ireland – partly for me I hoped. Beethoven's only opera "Fidelio" was chosen as a symbol of freedom, 150 years after its première at the nearby Theatre an der Wien during the French occupation.

In the morning an official ceremony was held in the auditorium still adorned in imperial gold and white; the famous white marble stairway had survived, and the classical paintings above it only had to be restored. Press from 27 countries watched from the first balcony as the Austrian chancellor entered with the new musical director, Dr. Karl Böhm. Then after formal welcoming speeches, he conducted Bach's tranquil air from the 'suite in D', and was handed the golden key to this phoenix risen from the ashes. He followed it with the overture to "The Mastersingers" and then unannounced, as though to trump its Germanic content, played "The Blue Danube."

Long before the performance began, the square in front was crowded, and later visitors arrived clutching their precious tickets when showing them at a police cordon. (When Emperor Franz Josef and his court arrived to attend the opening performance in 1869, scarcely any sightseers were in evidence – such is the proliferation of music since those days.)

The performance was televised for posterity, and visitors signed their names in a golden book for the theatre archives; it was believed to have then been the richest night in theatrical history - £39,000 being paid for the 2,100 seats – the thought that I was probably the poorest person there (in finance only) did not detract in the least from the event. As well as church and state dignitaries, the attendance included Bruno Walter, Shostakovich – not wearing the required evening dress – and composers Carl Orff, Werner Egk, Frank Martin, Rolf Liebermann and von Einem. Wieland Wagner I noticed down from Bayreuth, sitting next to American composer Menotti. Directors of more than twenty opera houses were also present.

The artists chosen for the great occasion – the opera was relayed from speakers placed around the Ringstrasse – were Martha Mödl as Leonora, Anton Dermota singing Florestan for the first time – Ludwig Weber as Rocco, and Paul Schöffler as Don Pizzaro. The orthodox production was by Heinz Tietjens. The third "Leonora" overture was played between the last two scenes as is customary, but applause ruined the effect as a bridge. (At Franz Josef's opening "Don Giovanni" half the audience left during the 'entertainment' which was very inadequately staged apparently.) The 500 standing tickets were sold to enthusiasts who had queued 70 hours; seats were bought at 75p to £70 each from a ballot giving only a 10/1 chance of success.

The following morning I decided to give thanks at the Royal Chapel where the famous Vienna boys' Choir were taking part in Beethoven's "Mass in C" unannounced, as is their duty. It was a most moving occasion, and I later visited their home at the Augarten Palace, where the oldest Viennese institution, founded in 1498, is now housed. Both Schubert and Haydn were among its early members. The choir is divided into many sections, which tour widely, and I had often heard them in London and in Ireland, sometimes in drag for comic operettas.

The other operas chosen for the festival were "Don Giovanni", Richard Strauss's "The woman without a shadow" conducted by his friend Karl Böhm, Verdi's "Aida", "The Mastersingers", "Der Rosenkavalier", and finally "Wozzeck" which I missed – without much regret. In the opera house, a beautiful new

82

drop curtain in red, gold and brown depicts Orpheus leading out Eurydice. It was raised the first morning to reveal 800 members of the Vienna State Opera seated high in the tiers. The stage is 50m deep and 45m high. "This house is devoted to all that is pure and noble", the spirit of Vienna recited at the opening in 1869, "May its halls never be closed by the noise of war". War came but it was overcome.

While there I also went to see the Spanish Court Riding School in their correct setting, but more importantly to an historically intriguing concert in the Rasumovsky Palace, where the present Count Rasumovsky attended as a minor music critic. But so did a descendant of Beethoven, a grey-haired lady to whom I was introduced, was married to the great-grandson of Beethoven's renegade nephew Karl. Rasumovsky quartets were played.

We were taken one day to Esterhazy Palace where Haydn worked for many years, though it was in great disrepair having been recently evacuated by Russian troops, who had even used ceiling cherubs for targets practise, and given it other gross insults. We saw, too, Haydn's home – terrible to think he had an unloving, unmusical wife – and the little church to which he had two funerals! Yes, his body was first taken there in 1809 minus its head, for some strange reason, and that became the prize trophy of the otherwise illustrious Viennese Music Society until 1954, when it was given a state funeral back to join the other remains.

The Royal Danish Ballet is not only one of the oldest in Europe, with a tradition dating back 200 years, but it is now one of the finest companies, although drawing dancers chiefly from a country no bigger than Ireland. My five annual visits to their spring festivals held during the second half of May when Denmark is awaft with the scent of lilac began in 1956. It is the only festival I might even visit again, so much did I enjoy the country and its amiable people.

Ballet and opera are staged in the Royal Danish theatre adjacent to the Nyhavn seamen's taverns, and the beautiful stage is surmounted by the motto: "Not only for pleasure". There I used to see King Frederick following scores in the royal box which he visited frequently and sometimes conducted in private; everywhere I was aware of important royal patronage. This was in marked contrast to the performance there with Queen Elisabeth in the royal box: she entered, and sat enduring the ballet, without a smile on her face all evening. Next day I was asked "Can the British Queen never smile in an opera house?"

George came there one year, too, and we went up to Hamlet's Elsinore Castle for a concert, and in that small town, too, I sometimes heard organ recitals of music by Buxtehude – much admired by Bach – who was born there in 1637.

Many works in the repertoire of the royal Danish Ballet are by their famous choreographer August Bournonville, often to music by H.C. Lumbye – the Danish Johan Strauss – and his associates. The company is noted, too, for the equally famous Danish Pantomime theatre that now plays in their own theatre with its curious peacock's tail drop-curtain that opens down the centre for an evening of free entertainment, like other events in Tivoli. There, too, I saw the new concert hall being opened in 1956 to replace the one wantonly blown up by retreating German soldiers.

Mozart operas are especially well staged there, though in Danish, as is the rule, possibly because his widow Constanze married a Danish diplomat, and the composer's works arrived there fast. The festival is held – or was forty years ago – during the last two weeks of May.

It used to be a very expensive city, though I learned how to take evasive action to save myself being unsettled by that statistic, but thankfully that matters less nowadays. During one of the early festivals I sat next to the director on a bus travelling north – perhaps I was wearing my dark-green suit that turned almost black in theatre lights – and he remarked as we passed Charlottenlund beach that I might very well find it a suitable place for swimming. I certainly did, after exploring within the flimsy screens that hid the men's nude bathing place spread out on wooden pontoons into deep water, perfect for relaxation and companionship.But I was saddened to hear only a week later that the director himself had evidently gone there and swum straight out to sea, drowning, for whatever reason.

Carl Nielsen, an exact twin of Sibelius, was the great Danish symphonist, and I had many chances to become better acquainted with his works during my visits, and also at the central island of Fünen where he was born at Odense. (His autobiography "My Childhood" gives a charming account of his early years in that lovely place, also the birthplace of the gay writer Hans Christian Anderson.) There I saw a charming little sculpture of the composer seated on a tree-stump playing pan-pipes by his wife, a noted sculptor whose Copenhagen tribute shows him riding naked on a horse . . . not far away from the notorious, ugly, Mermaid. In Odense I had also met two of his nieces at an all-Nielsen concert during the festival; he was for several years a member of the orchestra in the Royal Theatre. Finally I add one sour note. At a press conference I met Stravinsky, who was there to receive a very lucrative Danish musical award; I placed the fact beside the knowledge that he had once asked a friend of mine to pay about a pound for his autograph!

The music festival down at Aix-en-Provence in the south of France I visited twice by scooter, too, so that I could escape during the daytime down to Cassis, a pleasant Mediterranean resort. There I heard the great guitarist Segovia playing at an outdoor concert in the courtyard of the Bishop's Palace, an ideal setting for such gentle music, played to perfection. The Mozart opera standard was high, too, with notable designs often by Jean-Pierre Ponelle.

The festivals at Amsterdam were given in June, and also included performances at the Hague and Rotterdam since the Dutch will not drive the intervening thirty miles, causing an entire opera production to be repeated across country instead.

Concerts in the famous Concertgebouw were highlights, and afterwards I often retreated to the famous gay bar D.O.K. unique in its day – I paid about a pound for a 10-day membership card – and ticked off mentally the British music critics as they arrived without fail, some rather timidly. One critic said to me: "Gerard, fancy seeing you here!" to which I replied: "Well, when did you ever see me with a girl at Covent Garden?" Touché. Some years I stayed at the Kürhaus at Scheveningen, the pleasant resort where, however, many Dutch would not then go saying it was overrun by Germans. The sand dunes there were particularly pleasant for a stroll. .

Two more festivals I will briefly describe, those at Prades and Prague, very different from each other. The former was only held in my day at the small town near Perpignan in south-eastern France because the great 'cellist Pablo Casals had settled there teaching in his old age. I went down as part of a scooter "Tour de France" to watch the little master play again with his old enemy the pianist, Alfred Cortot, whom he had ignored for twenty years since they were joined by Jacques Thibaud as a celebrated trio, I was told. It was a lovely occasion given in a small church at night, well worth the long journey. I went to his home later to hear him give a master-class at which he welcomed kindly visitors from abroad.

But the next morning my adventurous spirit took a tumble. I noticed on my map that Andorra was only 50 miles away, and decided it would therefore make a perfect day's outing before leaving Prades. What I did not notice, however, was the colouring of my map that might have indicated a 50-mile hill! It was July, and I set off in shorts, as the weather was hot at sea level. I saw marvellous scenery as I drove continuous hairpin bends high and higher on my ever-reliable Lambretta, as I can now safely call it. But then it became colder fast, and just before I arrived at Andorra – spurred by the thought of cheap petrol, even for a scooter – it began to snow.

Then visibility closed in, and I turned round after entering the independent territory briefly, and rapidly descended to a more agreeable climate my teeth chattering en route.

The other festival at Prague was a very different matter. I decided to mark my 40th birthday by planning a trip to the Prague Spring Festival in late May by scooter – it surprises the young to hear I did not own a car until I was over forty. The Czech Embassy in London needed to know the registration number of my car, overwritten scooter, and where I would be staying each night so the Russians then in control of the charming old city could keep careful tabs on me, if deemed necessary.

I drove through the Bohemian forests in great delight, and saw may-poles erected, as for Smetana's opera "The Bartered Bride", but nearby I noticed megaphones on top of prominent houses presumably telling the villagers what to think. A gruesome sight. Then ultimately I saw a sign reading "Prague 5km" and thought how extraordinary that I could not see it. Suddenly I found I had come in on top of a plateau, and there below me in a vast trench lay the magnificent city; a wonderful sight, missed by those flying in direct.

The festival press had given me a hotel room and free tickets for any performances, including concerts by the famous Czech Philharmonic Orchestra, so I greatly enjoyed visiting them and the national Opera, and the smaller Opera where Mozart's "Don Giovanni" was first performed. The Czechs remained great admirers of Mozart and even looked after one of his sons after his death. I visited the lovely Bertramka Villa in which he completed the opera, and later saw the adjacent graves of Smetana and Dvorak in the Vysherad national cemetery.

Dvorak's birthplace, a butcher's shop not far from town, I visited more romantically with a young Czech ballet-master I had encountered in a crowd – such a thing can happen if you are lucky. Franticek, or my 'fancy Czech' as George later dubbed him, was very good company for my stay. He had been well off, but he and his mother were then living in a small apartment in what was formerly their own large house, taken over by the Russian authorities.

He asked me to take his mother for a spin on my scooter, since she had once owned a large car – a poor substitute I thought. Later she showed me an interesting volume of photos filled only with those taken of him every few months from birth until aged 27 – his beauty was adequate excuse.

One night he met me in the interval of the opera, to my surprise, holding a bottle of champagne, a treasure in a city where everyone then earned £7 a week whatever they did, he explained. We could not drink in the boulevard cafes, as the Russians would want to know how you could afford it.

He explained we would set off immediately after the opera to drive out the 15 miles to Kladno where he had digs as the ballet-master there. I first had to fetch my scooter from a subterranean garage in which I hid it on arrival since there were no other Lambrettas in Prague and I feared inquisitive young Czechs might break it.

After a very entertaining night, as you can imagine, he took me to watch him take a ballet class. On the way back we passed a most tragic place, Lidice, where the village was utterly razed to the ground by Nazis in a reprisal attack, killing about 300 inhabitants. It is now a vast rose garden with contributions from many different countries. A few years later he wrote to me in London to tell me he had since joined the East Berlin Opera Ballet, taking his mother there too. Later both had somehow escaped over, or through, the Berlin Wall into the West and he was then in Munich. Unfortunately I have heard no more, and have no address to write to.

My two visits to the Edinburgh festival warrant little comment. I attended the first festival, having scooted up from London with only one overnight stop. The second time I went by bus, an horrendous undertaking to my mind, that made me swear never to be encased so long again. The standard up there was all right, but scarcely up to international standards I thought, more especially since then they had no adequate opera house. I left it strictly alone afterwards; to have a huge 'fringe' of semi-amateur events is no adequate compensation.

From all those years at Covent Garden, hundreds of performances in all, I choose two very special occasions, Sir Thomas Beecham, by far my favourite British conductor, giving "The Mastersingers" at his 250th appearance in the great theatre, which on account of much intrigue he never actually directed, and it was the opera's 150th staging there. The other greatest occasion, since those early Flagstad "Tristan" evenings, was the complete Berlioz "The Trojans" staged there for the first time under Kubelik and produced by Sir John Gielgud. There is no greater combined music and spectacle in the repertoire.

In some ways the most unexpected of these musical occasions was the première at Sadler's Wells in June 1945 of Benjamin Britten's first opera "Peter Grimes", based on a poem by Crabbe, and set in an east coast English fishing village.

He and his lifelong friend Peter Pears, had spent several years together in America, and we were consequently unprepared for such a blazing masterpiece. In fact I doubt he ever surpassed it, though I went to all his subsequent operas, except the church parables, and his final "Death in Venice", by which time I was living again in Ireland. (I was told he was only given permission to use the Thomas Mann novella on condition he never saw the Visconti film.)

"Peter Grimes" is now rightly acclaimed as one of the 20th century's finest operas; its all embracing seascape, the lives of the fisherfolk, and local hostile reaction to Peter Grimes' solitary nature are brilliantly evoked. But more especially it is remarkable for the wonderful way Britten incorporated his own strong beliefs and visions.

For example, when the chorus declaims "We live and let live, we keep our hands to ourselves", his pacifism is to the fore, and when Ellen Orford, who befriends his new apprentice boy, sings "Here is a friend!" his Quaker background is asserted. There is aptness, too, in Grimes saying how he is "rooted there by familiar fields."

I attended almost all its early performances enthralled, and it suited the relatively small theatre much better than when later transferred to Covent Garden. Peter Pears sang the title role, as in all other Britten operas, and his singing as the evangelist at the time in Bach's "St. Matthew Passion" – albeit in English as was the post-war ruling – was excellent too. Especially opposite the matchless Kathleen Ferrier.

I cycled one evening after work to Wimbledon Town Hall to hear her London début recital, word of her amazing tonal quality having reached me in time. But her beautiful speaking voice, introducing the lieder, was a generous bonus; soon afterwards I had an opportunity to interview her. Dressed in a beautiful kimono, a tall stately figure, she chatted about her special interest in Mahler's music, and particularly his "The Song of the Earth" which she soon came to own on the London concert scene.

Naturally I went down to Glyndebourne occasionally where Mr. John Christie's classic opera-house stood adjacent to his lovely home near Lewes in the Sussex Downs, which was known as "a favourite haunt of the muses", even long ago. He opened it in 1935 for his wife Audrey Mildmay who first sang Susanna there in Mozart's "The Marriage of Figaro". In 1947 Kathleen Ferrier made her operatic début there in the first performance of Britten's "The Rape of Lucretia", his second opera. (Petrol rationing was still in force, and I had to scrounge an extra coupon to fill my motorbike for the drive down, changing into the obligatory evening dress behind a hedge when the estate came near.)

Peter Pears sang the male chorus, and Ferrier gave a superb display, vocally and in her acting, as Lucretia, with wonderfully sustained power and breath control; few singers assay the role today, and in consequence it remains a memorial, to a degree, to this very great singer. Fortunately I did not hurry from the theatre, unusually, and saw John Christie come on stage, visibly moved by the grandeur of the work, and heard him say: "This had been a Mozart theatre to date, but now we are pleased to welcome Benjamin Britten also". What an amazingly far-sighted accolade.

In later years I used to go down occasionally to enjoy the lovely fête champêtre, strolling in the gardens near the ha-ha sunken fence, or walking by the lake. Alas Felix Aprahamian, critic of "The Sunday Times", did not keep his idea of coming down pillion on my

90

motorbike with his opera cloak flying, and a picnic hamper balanced between us. That would have been something for Christie's pedigree cattle to observe, a "deus/x ex machina" worthy of the one I once saw descend from the clouds at Drottningholm Theatre near Stockholm.

From about ten other visits there I remember specially a week of Mozart concerts given by Sir Thomas Beecham, the ideal conductor and a wonderful production of Mozart's favourite among his operas, "Idomeneo".

In my early days I also enjoyed the crystal singing of the fine oratorio specialist, Isobel Baillie, and Heddle Nash's last performance as Gerontius, a part he virtually owned for several years. Other happy memories are of hearing Richard Tauber singing Don Ottavio with the Vienna State Opera, as a guest in London, a week before he died, and many evenings with Menuhin, Solomon, Dame Myra Hess or Clara Haskil.

My Britten sessions ended ideally when I attended the first performance of his masterly "War Requiem" in 1962 at the opening of Coventry's rebuilt cathedral, an act of true reconciliation between nations. St. Michael's Anglican cathedral, built in the perpendicular style about 1500AD was totally destroyed on November 14th 1940, in one of the worst air-raids. The new cathedral, built after six years' continuous work, has the bombed ruin incorporated into Sir Basil Spence's plan, adjoining the new in a most harmonious manner. "The new cathedral should grown from the old and be incomplete without it", he told me at the time. Many German specialists were assisting the great undertaking.

Its most notable decoration is Graham Sutherland's tapestry, then the largest in existence, hanging behind the high altar, showing "Christ in Glory", which took more than two years to complete at Aubusson, eight weavers using more than 1,000 colours. The Berlin Philharmonic took part in the festival which was crowned by the première of Britten's "War Requiem" sung by British, German and Russian soloists. The great sorrowful work, based on the terrible futility of war, quoted several war poets, and was immediately acclaimed world-wide.

When I heard "Messiah" - with its marvellous opening statement "Comfort ye my people" – aged 16, on a trip down to Dublin
from St. Columba's, I was virtually knocked out. So, too, when I
first encountered Haydn's "The Creation" in a London suburb; alas
his superb early oratorio "The Return of Tobias" (1775), currently
one of my favourite pieces, is now so very seldom heard. In the war,
too, I went to Golders Green to hear Bach's "Mass in B minor", and
an old gentleman, perhaps 50, turned to me and said: "Are you
about to hear this for the first time? Oh, you are so lucky!" I soon
knew what he meant.

I must mention, too, the Irish National Ballet's remarkable
work based on the life of Oscar Wilde, with music by Sir Arnold
Bax, which I saw premièred in Cork Opera House about ten years
ago, before the company was disbanded due to lack of financial support. I met Sir Arnold some years earlier when he was living at an
inn in Sussex, and held the virtually honorary post of "Master of the
Queen's Musick".

We talked about his close friendship with the Irish, especially in Cork, and in Connemara where he was cheerfully known as
"ould bags", as he related in his autobiography "Farewell My
Youth". But his music I have found difficult, and I was apprehen-
sive about its use. I need not have been; the score was apt, and a
delight.

The ballet managed to cover so many aspects of Wilde's fascinating life in great detail, I was astonished at its ingenuity. All the
central characters were present, and emphasis seemed very well
placed. For example Wilde's love for Bosie was powerfully shown
in some very simple brief pas-de-deux; the flashbacks to reality were
present at every step. How succinct, for example, was Wilde's
action when he strolled by a young lad standing under a lamppost
and just raised his hat with his cane to obtain a better view. But
most impressive of all was the moment when music no longer suf-
ficed, as in Beethoven's ninth symphony, and we heard declaimed:
"The love that dare not speak its name". The ballet was video-ed,
so I hope it is not lost forever.

The career of the great German baritone, Dietrich Fischer-

Dieskau I followed closely right from 1951, when I saw his London début conducted by Sir Thomas Beecham, so supreme in Delius, in the composer's "Mass of Life", a surprising choice for the occasion. Few were present in the Albert Hall, but it was unforgettable.

Through the years I saw him giving wonderful performances, especially as the Count in Mozart's "The Marriage of Figaro" at the Salzburg Festival, dressed in leather, lord of all he surveyed, and at Bayreuth as Wolfram in "Tannhäuser", giving a singing lesson to the others in the first act septet. There were also his towering evenings there as the "Flying Dutchman".

Once I drove my scooter to Oxford to see Sir Thomas give the rarely staged Delius opera "Irmelin" on a Saturday afternoon. He entered the university's Sheldonian theatre, almost empty, with an expression that so clearly said: "A pearl before swine!" But he was undeflected in his personal joy, as I was.

Finally I recall Maria Callas whom I saw about 15 times at Covent Garden, usually on second nights since I always insisted on writing delayed notices for "The Irish Times", allowing time for reflection, such as was the practice in the 19th century. Too often I read ill- written snap reports by critics who had telephoned from outside the theatre.

I first heard her in Bellini's "La Sonnambula" at an early Edinburgh Festival, and her brilliant display as Amina remained her best interpretation to my mind, young though she then was. Later I greatly admired her acting, but she was not one of my favourite singers; her recordings I liked better than her stage appearances, but who can say whether they were not technically manipulated.

Anyhow my order of preference subsequently was her "Lucia di Lammermoor", then "Tosca" opposite Tito Gobbi, a very formidable Scarpia, and her tragic, sorrowing "La Traviata". I also saw her in "Norma" and Cherubini's "Medea". Knowledge of her strange turbulent, and later tragic, life may have affected my judgement. Too much essayed in life, perhaps; a comet burned in a flash. Once I saw her in Bellini's "Norma" with the very young Joan Sutherland, who ultimately took over many of her roles. I preferred her tone to that of Maria Callas, but alas her acting was minimal in stark contrast. Indeed, these two famous singers never replaced Elizabeth Schwarzkopf, especially in Mozart and Richard Strauss, in my estimation.

Chapter eight

Finland and Sibelius

Coming back from Germany one summer I chanced to sit opposite a young man who told me much about the magic of Finland from which he was returning. Avoiding their winter and its eternal night, he had gone there during the summer when the sun just dips to the horizon at midsummer and immediately rises again. He spoke of its 60,000 lakes, pine trees contrasting beautifully with silver birch, and every home possessing a sauna from which you would run naked into the nearby lake or the sea. In winter you roll in the snow before returning to the furnace to continue chatting to your host before dinner. Saunas originated in Finland, and are used there for hospitality, and as complete levellers of rank. No Finn would ever carry a towel therein, only bunches of birch twigs with which to beat yourself, or others. I was immediately hooked on the idea of seeing this fascinating place, especially since their great symphonist Sibelius had long been one of my favourite composers.

A Sibelius Festival was held in Helsinki each summer at which all the composer's seven symphonies were played, usually in chronological order, as well as many of his romantic symphonic poems.

The first time I went by ship from Copenhagen to Turku, and then on by train to Helsinki, passing through a Russian enclave, Porkkala, en route where shutters were slammed ignominiously across the carriage windows in case passengers glimpsed the forbidden land. A puerile effort indeed. Otherwise we passed through immense forests, and saw trees growing seemingly straight out of granite outcrops. In the distance smoke coiled aloft from sauna fires, so numerous that one could often smell the burning pinewood drifting across the lake. I seem to smell it still . . .

In London it so happened that the Finnish Embassy's cultural attaché's son, Klaus Solanko, was studying in Helsinki, and became my guide to that wonderful place where modern architecture is so honoured. He was studying it luckily, so I had the ideal guide to its finest examples and merits in and around the capital. Alvar Altonen's work I liked especially, and I noted the way the

Finns always build houses around established trees, never interfering with their own innate grandeur. Near Helsinki, too, is a church where the altar is placed at the side giving a view of the forest priority for the worshippers; one does not easily forget such considerations.

I was reporting on the Sibelius Festival not only for "The Irish Times" but also for other papers including the London "Times" which, incidentally rewarded me with two guineas for half a column. Papers have little respect for young journalists' capabilities as I learned long ago. Klaus was musical, too, and would rush over to tell me whether or not all five of Sibelius's daughters were present that evening in the great University Hall where several of his works were first performed.

The festival atmosphere was convivial. I spoke to one young American who admitted he had camped outside Sibelius's home, the Villa Ainola, 19 miles from Helsinki in the forest in the hope of catching a glimpse of the aged composer who had not, in fact, been into Helsinki for more than 15 years, but sat with his beloved wife Aino listening to his works broadcast from afar. Sometimes he would send a telegram of approval or otherwise.

Members of visiting orchestras would occasionally be invited out there briefly and might be acknowledged from the window while standing on the lawn. Although he was living on a large state pension, he had not composed for more than 30 years, and never received guests, I heard.

At a press conference I met an interesting Finnish composer Yrjo Kilpinen who had composed more than 600 songs, and was a good friend of Richard Strauss, about whom he told me much. On another evening I went to a reception given by their well-known conductor Hannikainen, where, alas, I had the sad spectacle of seeing his son, about 30, being fed by his mother, having suffered a stroke when deserted by his wife. Their best-known pianist also invited me out to his forest home, where he talked about the wealth of Sibelius's piano music, which remains virtually unknown in the west, but in which his development is as clear as in the symphonies.

The Helsinki harbour front is a superb expanse with the

Russian Orthodox Church with its onion tower overhanging from on high. Florists sell flowers there but in small quantities as are given where the summer months quickly pass. Their notable glass industry sells chiefly specimen vases, and a single rose – as I was given by a handsome young companion – is the recognised farewell.

The Helsinki swimming pools were well patronised with adjacent saunas into which one escaped high summer temperatures, leaving swimming trunks outside. They consider it rude to talk loudly, or to eat, within their honoured bathhouses. In some they employ old crones, over 40 by law, to beat your back with twigs. This I could not escape once, speaking no Finnish, and file it away among my oddest memories.

Another time I returned to the Helsinki Festival taking the comfortable Swedish boat from Stockholm to Helsinki for the memorable experience of seeing the capital rise out of the sea before your eyes as you approach, skirting a maze of small islands.

But the last of my four visits to Finland was the most exciting, as it was mid-winter. Klaus's father arranged through their Embassy for me to go on a Finnish ship from Hull to Helsinki, a five-day voyage. I was the only passenger, and was served excellent food at the captain's table. At times the sea was very rough which I enjoy; the radio in my cabin flew across the room, drawers flew open, too. As we passed Copenhagen I saw its beautiful spires and in some ways wanted to see it all again.

Klaus greeted me in a frozen January Helsinki. It was about minus three, but as he explained that temperature feels colder than about minus thirty in Lapland away from the sea. Young Finns skied by on the streets and pavements while I slithered along uncertainly. I watched ice hockey, bought muffs to protect my ears when it became even colder, and a fur hat. I even tried fishing through holes in the ice, as a novelty, but nought came up to greet me.

One day as Klaus and I walked around the offshore islands through the snow, we came upon people ice yachting, and he stopped one and asked the owner to please give his Irish friend a spin. Lying flat, my face inches from the ice, the speed seemed fantastic: but at least I had tried it. He also pointed out another curious form of transport, a potkukelka, which is a kitchen chair on runners on which you push the young – practical in the extreme if you keep your own balance meanwhile.

I had gone to Finland in January wanting to see a reindeer round-up in Lapland close at hand. Soon I flew north with a journalist from Israel and a member of their tourist office, acting as host. I wore my father's old full-length leather motorcycling coat, and on arrival in Lapland was loaned a pair of reindeer skin one-piece leg boots that are advisable in temperatures of about minus 45° which we soon encountered.

The flight from Helsinki to Ivalo, their terminus 200 miles north of the arctic circle took about three hours, touching down at Oulu and Rovaniemi, the most devastated area in Europe in 1944 when utterly destroyed by Germans refusing to retreat. On arrival we continued our journey by taxi over hard-packed snow at great speed, so used to these conditions are the drivers using chains, despite a road sign warning of bends for the next 20 kilometres. Upturned boats seemed odd by the roadside, as we sped along.

On our arrival at Inari, a small community on the western bank of Lake Inari, centre of the Finnish Lapps, we heard much about their way of life. Although there were then only about 2,400, they enjoyed full rights  and protection as an independent minority. (There are 10,000 Lapps in Sweden and 20,000 in Norway, where most people tending reindeer are loosely termed Lapps.)

Only our Lake Inari Lapps wear the colourful four-pointed "Hats of the Four Winds" in blue, red and yellow. In wintertime the full costume is worn regularly and never merely donned for visitors who, in any case, are very few.

There were, in fact, no other guests that January in the newly designed tourist hotel, since no one could yet ski, the snow being too dry and powdery. Also most Finns believe, as do foreigners, that it is totally dark in northern Lapland at that time of the year. But actually we had daylight from 10:00 to 4:00, and about two hours of sunshine daily.

In March there are reindeer races on Lake Inari before it becomes one of Europe's finest fishing areas. Only by looking at photographs on the hotel walls did I realise it overlooked a fine salmon fishery. Also reindeer, fascinating creatures that they are, refuse to race against each other, and have to be timed separately. I was amused to hear of the tourist who set forth for a leisurely drive in a reindeer pulkka sled but arrived back considerably bruised having been harnessed to a racer. The husky dogs I loved, playful creatures who sometimes, however, are killed when they charge a car, so infrequently seen, believing it to be some kind of fast-moving animal.

We took the post bus next day on a newly opened road to Utsjoki, the most northerly village in Finland; many Lapps were in it and their costumes made colourful company. I never expected to see "hats of the four winds" quivering above seats in a small modern bus. Their reindeer-skin shoes had quaintly curved toes, and some wore fur coats beautifully made from young reindeer pelts.

One Lapp spoke good English, perhaps learned from English fishermen – or a lover – in summer months, and told me he recently took a 65lb salmon "on a real Devon bait". He said he had learned English in addition from "Time" and "Country Life" to which he subscribed.

Ptarmigan we ate that night, reindeer tongues that were superb and local salmon kept in their natural deep-freeze. A short walk at -35° followed, though our guide suggested we try to learn skiing through the forests, a favourite Finnish pastime. I declined the offer, my nostrils already freezing over, my earmuffs hardening, and quickly beat a retreat to their sauna for more stories about the Lapps.

Later I met two young Finnish teachers in the hotel foyer, eager to improve their English, and they invited me to supper at their forest school. Beforehand, as courtesy there demands, I was taken to their sauna furnace with its marvellous aroma of pinewood and birch twigs. Soon bearing the heat no longer, we leapt out gaily rolling in the snow: overhead there happened to be a magnificent display of "northern lights" flashing across the pine forest as seen often at that high latitude.

We walked to church next day, about three miles, where the service was conducted in a small wooden parish hall built for the 1,100 members of the Evangelical Lutheran community. In the evening we visited the Lapp High School at which 20 girls and 10 boys were studying, aged 16 to 23 on a single six-month course. There is much competition for admittance, so pupils cannot be retained longer. The head-master told us he tries then to open up some intellectual future for his pupils, encouraging them to continue studying when they return to their wandering Lapp community, or go south to a technical school.

"What shall we tell our visitors now?" he asked his pupils, some very beautiful lads among them. "About the poro, reindeer" they called out laughing. For the early spring round up was about to take place; they wished they were coming with us next day, when I would have my odd ambition fulfilled.

In 1830 there were still reindeer in central Finland, but now they remain in the farthest north where they number about 150,000. (They have been introduced into Scotland quite successfully in recent years, also). The best are worth about £18 each, so a man with 200 is quite well off. But one may never inquire how many anyone has; it is like asking a neighbour about his bank account.

When we arrived at Petsikko, on the fells, about 3,000 reindeer were gathered in a large corral, having been rounded up from the wildest regions by men with huskies, then worth about £100 each, and doing the work of several men. It was altogether a magnificent sight, with snow dust, and steam from the crowded animals, grunting loudly, glinting in the low sunshine, enhanced by the colourful costumes of some 200 Lapps taking part.

Before long we bravely entered the corral, and the editor of a Lapp paper, showed us how to lasso a reindeer. Soon I had one caught by the antlers, having stood my ground while hundreds appeared to charge but carefully divided – as did the Red Sea – when they reached me. Over it went struggling in the snow; the editor pounced on it and examined its ears for identification. Soon he himself had blood around his mouth, having bitten a mark on the captive's ear. Reindeer will not bite in return. Lapps are kind to them. Laughter not anger, filled the corral; if a reindeer refuses to start on a journey with a pulka sled, it is considered unlucky to force it to obey.

They feed on lichen in the winter – I hope the terrible Chernobyl radiation has not killed many since my visit – and drink the snow. So it is not allowed to pursue them for more than 35 minutes at a time; then they must rest. They may not be kept in a corral for more than two days, when the next batch appear. An area can only sustain a certain number, which their association fixes, and a tax man hovers nearby noting how many each Lapp possesses if he can, but they are understandably very lightly taxed.

At midday we went into a low wooden hut – the Lapps are mostly very short – for a meal of reindeer soup, reindeer flesh and potatoes. Vegetables are very expensive up north, and oranges are eaten instead. No alcohol was seen, unusual for Finland. Bread made from reindeer brains I did not try to my knowledge. Those animals that are slaughtered are taken away from their companions' sight for the purpose.

Wolves seldom enter Finland from Russia, whence expected naturally, but some Lapps obtain riches most cruelly by finding where a big bear is sleeping out the winter and selling the information for as much as £300 to foreign hunters who then shoot it as it awakes, a most ghastly form of treachery.

On my return to Helsinki Klaus Solanko introduced me to Jussi Jalas, conductor at the Finnish National Opera, and a son-in-law of Sibelius, the greatest symphonist of his day, it was usually agreed. Klaus told him how much I liked Finland and saw it through my great love of Sibelius's music. Indeed Klaus's parents had once remarked: "Do borrow our country house in central Finland, if you wish; you'll know the scenery well, it has the arid, wild beauty of the fourth symphony . . ."

Mr. Jalas greatly admired Britten's operas and had translated some of the early ones for their Opera. He invited me to use the directors' box at the small, wooden National Finnish Opera, built in Russian style with very good acoustics. I remember the strange experience of hearing "Rigoletto" and "The Magic Flute" there sung in Finnish not, I thought, an inherently musical language. But in pre-war days a Finnish singer Aino Rautawaara was one of Glyndebourne's stars, and in recent times Matti Talvela, a true Nordic giant, has excelled abroad.

So it was with great delight that I accepted Jussi Jalas's invitation to go out with him in January 1957, to have coffee with

Sibelius, about six months before he died. I knew that the great composer, as well as being a connoisseur of cigars receiving many from admirers far and wide, was a fastidious dresser, so I set off through the deep snow to a clothier, picked at random. Great was their surprise when I told them I needed to be suitably attired to meet Sibelius; certainly my father's battered leather coat would be very inappropriate. My request made them leap in the air, since no-one from abroad had penetrated the sanctum of "Villa Ainola" for many years, except Sir Thomas Beecham when he had conducted for the first time in Helsinki at the last Sibelius summer festival. (One Finnish paper had shown the great Sibelian authority conducting at rehearsal with a baton in one hand and a sandwich in the other. I wonder had he ever before encountered an orchestra, like the Helsinki City Orchestra, led by a left-handed violinist?)

It had been the mildest winter there for thirty years, and the January snow lay lightly as we drove out the twenty miles northwards to Järvenpaa – the end of the lake – where stood Finland's most celebrated home, the "Villa Ainola", named after the composer's wife, Aino Järnefelt. It stood in a small wood overlooking a large lake, one of the country's loveliest, it was said.

On the way out Mr. Jalas told me I might write about my visit, but please not mention that he had again been very ill. He knew I would not ask the long-forbidden question, as to whether an eighth symphony existed in part, or complete. (No part of it was found after his death.) He also warned me, knowing I was particularly interested in opera, not to ask his father-in-law what he had achieved in that direction, since when someone dared to ask about his early attempt "The Maiden in the Tower", he earned the quick reply: "Leave her there!" (Yet I do have a tape of a studio broadcast of the work that shows merit, if little aptitude for the medium.)

The couple settled at the Villa Ainola in 1904. Sibelius remarking: "It was necessary for me to get away from Helsinki. My art demanded another environment. In Helsinki all melody died within me". He had not even visited the capital for about 17 years, so I was told, but remained deeply interested in all aspects of his art.

Eventually we came to a narrow avenue leading down to the villa, its red roof just visible between the snow-clad birch trees. It was built by the eminent architect Lars Sonck, who also designed the fine Kallio Church in Helsinki for which Sibelius wrote chimes in return. (I contrasted the Villa Ainola with the very simple house I had seen at Tavastehus, where Sibelius was born, and the woods in which as a young man, the composer "extemporised to the birds", hoping to become a concert violinist.)

On arrival, we paused to look across the lake, my host pointing out various details, but were soon called in to the drawing room where Sibelius was waiting to greet us. I saw a figure, shorter than I had expected, with those noble features, and broad introspective forehead. Then while drinking coffee and sampling cigars, he spoke of his visits to England, where he first went in 1905. He dedicated a symphony to Granville Bantock, and was President of the society honouring his friend Sir Arnold Bax. On hearing I came from Ireland, he showed me, from cases full of honours, a statue of St. Cecilia, patron saint of music, given to him by the Catholic Guild in 1950.

Later we spoke of Ireland's wealth of folklore, and Sibelius compared it briefly with that of Finland, which I had encountered only through a careful reading of their wonderful epic saga the "Kalevala". Sibelius drew on its very many runes depicting heroes such as Lemminkainen, in a most graphic manner. With what interest must he have discussed folk music with Sir Arnold Bax, who once call him: "An arresting formidable-looking fellow born of dark rock and northern forests".

Sibelius still took much interest in the music of his young contemporaries, recognising that they had difficulty sometimes establishing reputations in his shadow. In view of this he suggested that each festival in Helsinki should include music by younger composers, that I often attended.

He spoke of his great regard for Sir Thomas Beecham's interpretations of his music; he had heard his first Helsinki concert, comprising the last two symphonies that I had attended six months earlier. Many Finns told me they had never heard such fine playing from their orchestra as under his spell. (Naturally I did not presume to ask his opinion of various interpretations through the years, but when I mentioned I had had the good fortune to hear the great young French violinist Ginette Neveu playing his violin concerto just before she was killed in an air disaster, he spoke most highly of her recording of the music.)

I mentioned that unfortunately I had very seldom heard any of his piano music in London recitals, but that I had met its chief exponent at one of the Sibelius festivals, who had invited me out to

104

his country home and there, along with a few other guests, I had listened enthralled while he gave us a long recital of Sibelius piano music, introducing each piece, and showing how the composer's development can be followed in these works as clearly as in the symphonic music, once they are fully understood. Later he kindly sent me a book he had written on Sibelius piano music, which I have since lent to pianists, hoping that they may explore this part of the great man's output.

When he asked what other places I had visited in Finland, I told him how I had just returned from the Koli heights in Eastern Finland and in doing so had encountered graphic realisations of two of his symphonic poems. On the outward journey the bus, being driven through snow drifts in places, was nearing my destination at about eleven o'clock in the evening, when the driver asked me to alight at a junction, saying another bus would pick me up, fifteen minutes later, to take me to my hotel. Off it went. So there I stood in a dark Finnish forest, just as depicted in "Tapiola", in a very low temperature, watching for the predicted arrival of the special hotel bus: its lights soon appeared to my considerable relief. Three days later it was still dark when I left early in the morning. This time the car sped through the forests exactly as in "Night-Ride and Sunrise", until the dawn appeared.

As we were leaving, after I had been shown the simple but artistically arranged dining room and library, Sibelius turned and said: "Yes, small rooms, but here small themes grow large", referring engagingly to his very personal style of composition in which small whiffs of themes unite in splendour.

On fine days, he and his wife – whom I did not meet – still strolled in the garden, looking forward to visits from one or other of their five daughters. This time he did not venture out understandably, but Mr. Jalas showed me the garden, peeping out through light snow, and woods including an extra part bought for their master by the choral societies of Finland on his 60th birthday. So I left the man whose symphonies Rosa Newmarch once described as "A range of seven mountains rooted in the soil of one country, unified therefore in a basic sense, but extraordinarily diversified in contour and altitude".

A few days after this memorable meeting I left Kotka, their most easterly port in a small Finnish cargo boat. This time I was not alone, however; in the bus to Kotka I noticed a young Finn with exceptionally long blonde hair, unusual there, and was agreeably surprised to find the captain had placed us in the same smart cabin for the journey to London, where he was coming to learn English. The four days passed amusingly in his company, writing up some articles as well as enjoying excellent food on board.

It was a strange experience leaving a Finnish port in mid-winter; I had seen women loading the heaviest timber on board the boat with a crew of about twenty men, making sure the port was kept open as long as possible if the weather turned more severe. I saw carts and horses on the ice as we passed close-by through a myriad glistening islands that m ake great knowledge – or the service of a pilot – essential in summer months.

Just as we reached the entrance to the Thames, we entered heavy fog, and were stranded a full day almost within hailing distance of the shore. Much as I liked the mournful foghorns, I was worried of course by the thought of being a day late arriving back to George, and the inability of speaking meanwhile to him on the phone.

I suppose I was always too hard up to phone him from abroad; oddly enough I cannot recall ever having done so. But he dwelt so completely in my heart, as he well knew, wherever I was I felt accompanied by him, and guarded by him, as at this very moment. But I had never been late returning before, even if I arrived home to find him banished off engineering in Birmingham or elsewhere.

When we finally arrived in London docks I heard a crewmember call out in farewell: "Hey, why didn't you join us, during the voyage, in the ship's sauna?" He suggested a lost opportunity, naturally to be laughed at with George, the following day. The captain kindly stopped his car to give me a lift up from London's dockland. My cabin-mate came to a concert the following week, and there the memory fades.

Chapter nine

Restoring Thornfields
I do not know how many prospective buyers were shown Thornfields by my agents in 1963 when we decided to try and sell the house and lands; but consider what they saw. The front gate was painted dark green over layers of rust, the avenue was half of its present width, and had a central ridge in places on which weeds grew, since cars could only keep in one track causing numerous large potholes. A rusty iron boundary fence came within about ten feet of the avenue on the left-hand side approaching the little bridge painted white, again over rust. There one could scarcely glimpse the charming stream, since laurels and other scrub abounded. No lawn existed. We had not even owned a handsaw in my youth

As one approached the house, extensive briars coiled on either side, through which daffodils peeped pathetically in the spring. It was impossible to enter the walled garden from the avenue. Trees grew out of its long walls, and ivy hung almost to the ground.

Then the potential customer, already disillusioned I imagine, saw the huge mansion looking woebegone and foreboding. The window frames were painted dark green, with surrounding plasterwork falling away from damp, caused partly by ivy and virginia creeper growing to the roof. The shoots were also green, and leaked in many places from having a one-piece wooden ladder slammed against them whenever partly cleaned to little effect.

In the courtyard, superficially smart since the tenants had only thought of horses, there was one of our biggest beech trees, so rotten at the base, you could have bedded two dogs therein. They had even taken the liberty of breaking down an outhouse window, and removing its stonework, to admit yet another horse. Many stable doors were eaten away by boxer dogs they had once tried to breed there so inhumanely. In the garden one saw only a sea of dock which even horses refuse to eat. The roof of an old stable block, with a spacious harness-room, was about to collapse. Upstairs, if one ventured there as I did when a child, one was in danger of falling through the sagging floor. In a corner thrown among hay remnants dating from the governor's time, Thornfields' last farmer, was a beautiful white memorial tablet to his dear wife Betsy taken down from Stradbally Church when her name was added to his tablet in 1855. It frightened me as a child.

The potential buyer would then venture briefly inside, especially since there was not even a proper lock on the front door. Very good furniture, mostly in disrepair, stood around forlornly, many pieces bleached by the sun or chipped. All the woodwork was dark brown or black since Victorians overpainted only by adding darker stains and the house had not been decorated this century. We confirmed this by finding scribbled under the first of many old wallpapers on a bedroom wall: "It is 1887, I am Tom Ryan, being paid 4d hourly. Who are you?" Or words to that effect.

In the library on the left were about 2,000 books dating from the first half of the 19th century, the governor's working library. Many had very fine leather bindings and none had suffered dampness since the house at least was always dry. There were complete long runs of "The Delphin Classics" in Greek, "The Edinburgh Review" and the "Annual Register" to name but a few – once we rounded them up, and placed them in order, scattered as they had been all over the house.

But the visitor saw instead a very dangerous fireplace, with broken tiles at the side, and holes beneath leading down to the basement, from which a wind was supposed to aid the timid flames, entering from a broken window. In reality ash fell down, fortunately onto a tiled floor beneath. There was an attempt at electric light in that room only; there was one fuse in which lodged a piece of minor paling wire, to my horror. Outside in the shelter of a large beech tree stood amid the bamboos, an old wind-charger that someone meanly persuaded my father to buy in my absence. I doubt it ever provided any light even on the windiest nights, so snugly positioned.

Opposite the study was the main drawing room with chintz curtains c.1855 hanging from elegant giltwood pelmets festooned with cobwebs, on an ancient traction system. Every chair lacked upholstery, and the place stank from unattended animal droppings.

By this time I imagine the potential buyer was ready to flee, or perhaps he briefly ventured up the main stairs with walls painted in blue distemper that flowed with condensation much to the detriment of paintings hanging thereon. The brass stair-rods were all present, luckily, but black. A bedroom or two may have been shown – I doubt the only distant bathroom was – but probably not a spare-room in which the ceiling hung perilously in a curve, just about to collapse. The visit would then have quickly ended. Soon I was told that £3,000 was the highest offer, presumably for demolition; £13,000 I probably would have accepted. So very nearly came the demise of Thornfields again. So after much deliberation, we decided to try and save it, and I returned alone from London in May in my mini car loaded with possessions, and stayed at my sister's place at Bruff, Co. Limerick visiting the house which at least the tenants had vacated when asked to do so. I walked in the woods littered with baked-bean tins and broken bottles, and I think I was entitled to shed a tear at the prospect that lay ahead.

George was to arrive a month later, having seen his own furniture and possessions safely into a removal van. So the house would, in fact, stay empty for a month which it had never done before however unsatisfactory the tenants. For example the first in 1953 had signed a lease for £500 p.a. for five years, and then shortly afterwards said he was unwell and had to leave for South Africa, where he could not be sued for personal debt. My inefficient solicitor was totally unable to enforce his expensive lease against him.

The first thing I thought to do was to paint the front gate on the theory that passers-by would therefore think the place was still inhabited. A break-in would have been exceptionally easy, since two or three window frames had even been stolen complete. The good Meissen porcelain I had stored meanwhile at my sister's place, breaking some pieces in transit. My mother had naturally taken good small furniture for her bungalow on the understanding it was all to return to Thornfields ultimately.

Our beautiful red-and-white boxer pup watched me painting the front gate waiting for his other master. Timber, or Tim, we named him for our 20-acre overgrown estate. It was marvellous to see George soon again, but I felt dreadful taking him away from London his home city he liked so much. Yet he assured me he was fully ready for the undertaking.

It took about two months for his container to arrive; meanwhile we put new beds on piles of books in lieu of frames. Iron bedsteads, so wanted today, we flung out since we agreed smart tenants would require modern furniture. Out too went an antique clawfoot bath in which my mother bathed me so lovingly if the water was hot enough from the distant kitchen range. Ejected also was an even older bath made of flags, probably 18th century, we found in the garden filled with liquid manure. We had little time to pause for adequate research.

There were lean-to sheds for farm machinery outside the back garden wall, including a potting shed; these we demolished later for the slates badly needed for repairs to Limerick's St. John's Square roofing. We had to seek money in such odd ways. £2.50 had seemed much for our first blowlamp, I recall. We sought no grants in the knowledge that the money given would be soon clawed back in higher rates.

At first on windy nights the noise was terrible. Even our pup seemed frightened when doors banged wildly downstairs. All the original door furniture and mortise locks were broken; few door handles worked properly. George the engineer was very badly needed to repair them all in due course, and even spot matching new intricate doorplates in a job lot for a pound.

There were jackdaws' nests in almost all the 35 chimneys. All rooms, even in the large basement dating from about 1775 had fireplaces, except the empty wine cellar. Few chimneys ran direct. We even unblocked a bad pile-up behind the breast of the important drawing room fireplace by using a cannon-ball on the end of a rope.

Access to the attic was always a major problem since only I fitted through the small trap door, and larger George was mercifully spared from ever going there. What a place, enormous and open-plan. Traversing it so very often, I had to go on my knees over rafters, since duck-boards were very few, stooping low to avoid internal shoots and tanks, all by torchlight.

George, who had cooked so excellently in London by gas, was here confronted with electricity – of a sort. When we bought our first new electric cooker the grill would scarcely glow, due to the grossly inadequate supply delivering only 180 volts as was seen, when we insisted on having it measured. Luckily I had studied electricity as part of my physics course in TCD, so I determined to electrify the whole house myself, allowable at the time. I kept full records of my work on graph paper, and used correct ESB specification parts, bought wholesale. I even installed the fuse-boards. Each of our three six-room self-contained flats had to be on its own electrical circuit.

In the end we electrified the whole house perfectly, and with ample outlets, for about £400, whereas if done professionally it would have cost at least £4,000. Also electricians would have wrecked our ancient floorboards in their haste, and certainly not replaced them properly. We soon became expert with jemmies, just as George knew from arranging exhibitions at Olympia exactly how to move very heavy items on a system of rollers. But he knew everything it seemed; I never knew whether I admired or loved him the more!

We had to replace every sash-cord in the house, which we did singly when we restored each room. We also restored all the pine shutters, mostly not opened all my life, realising how important they are for heat conservation and security. (George was aghast once when I suggested not polishing the backs quite so carefully since they would only be revealed at dusk – no short cuts allowed.)

The walls were in such disrepair from people hanging pictures on large nails, that we used wallpaper invariably. Mostly we bought 'seconds', often with Georgian stripes which suited the house well. The big diningroom took sixteen rolls, more if we had chosen a patterned paper, since we only had three drops from a roll. Paper hanging was also George's forte, no imperfections went unseen but high work was left to me.

We could not afford scaffolding so I even papered ceilings occasionally off a single plank. For whom but George would I have gone up to the shoots so many times, or climbed among the chimney pots? (But think how those Roman soldiers, in olden times, fought so very bravely beside their lovers.)

Cleaning out the shoots was an essential horrible task; even if we could have afforded to pay a workman, how could we tell the job was properly done. Any small remaining obstruction was vital, especially since there was only one downpipe on account of the former necessity for saving rainwater for internal lead tanks.

While George anxiously held the ladder, muck fell on his lovely black hair. The slates, furthermore, had edged lower in places so it was impossible to put your hand into the O-gee shoots without the risk of being trapped atop a ladder. Access holes I had to make, carefully chipping away rough edges.

As we restored each room we usually took in the large pine window frames and removed the plate-glass carefully – glazing defeated us, as did good plastering. Then we would blow-lamp the frame, correctly undercoat after sanding by hand – George insisted electric sanders clog – and only then apply our final white gloss paint still perfect today. Sometimes I even had to blowlamp from high on a ladder. Only once did I nearly set the place on fire with the infernal machine; we found a room smoke-filled when we returned from lunch one day.

George was so ingenious, too; that sagging ceiling in an important spare-room he solved brilliantly, I thought, whereas it would have been difficult and costly to replace it. He noticed where many cracks merged, and there inserted metal plates about 4" square which he screwed back to the rafters lifting the original ceiling into place at no expense whatsoever.

One very pleasant surprise was the fact that all the woodwork was best pine and therefore almost unattacked by woodworm. The resin was still fresh wherever we had to cut. Also from about fifty window frames we only found one that needed a reinforcing corner bracket, so perfectly had the old lead paint protected them.

But another horror we met very unexpectedly when we took all the furniture out of a very large bedroom directly overhead the main drawingroom, preparing it for tenants. When we walked to the centre of the totally empty room, the floor shook ominously; would it in fact collapse? Luckily we happened to mention the fact to our excellent furniture restorer, Tom O'Connor, near Plassy. He told us to lift some floorboards and see whether the wedges between the joists had shifted. We had never seen such things; but exactly as he predicted, large heavy ones had somehow come adrift, whereas they are essential for tightening up such very long joists.

When we became tired of blowlamping with paraffin, unable to afford the gas type, and finding any proprietary paint-remover would scarcely blister our ancient foe, we would go out into the woods, play about, and cut ivy off more trees. We both detested it, often as thick as our wrists, and had to remove wide sections to destroy it permanently. I might cut briars, too, with a scythe, but since that only pruned them, soon took to digging up the roots instead.

Ultimately we had the garden ploughed and removed dock in barrow loads, but did not have it harrowed and consequently it remained unpleasantly ridged in places. As if that was not enough we discovered much scutch-grass in the soil and had to remove it by hand, clearing a patch the size of a tennis court which we then defended from rabbits with chicken wire, before growing vegetables and some flowers. Scarlet runner beans, gladioli and black-currants rewarded us best. George would make jam from the vast crop on twelve bushes we bought initially for a pound. But alas sometime cattle would be seen sitting on our chosen patch since farmers were then allowed to let them roam the land; it was illegal to guide them casually out your gate, those sacred cows!

Meanwhile we kept Tom O'Connor busy with furniture restoration; at the auction about fifteen years later people commented on the fine general condition. The first item we took him was once a superb Georgian bow-fronted mahogany chest of drawers that looked ready for our dump, but came back in pristine condition. He loved working on really good pieces, and never over-restored ruining the patinas. Furthermore he always went "easy with the ink", as he called it charmingly. We learned never to ask for an estimate of time or price; we grew to trust him implicitly, and he knew we were not reselling his work that he would often see admired by all. A real craftsman, and so vital to our overall plan.

We attacked the study straight away to make ourselves a snug, and decided to remove two protruding bookcases to increase the size to very nice proportions. In one my father had once removed a row of books to make an aviary in which canaries bred to my delight. We kept only one very nice rope-edged mahogany inset bookcase. For the broken fireplace George remembered the tablet to Betsy thrown out in the hay. We took off the grey marble backing that exactly made a base in front, completely safe, and put broken pieces of matching grey and white marble where the Victorian tiles had been. The tablet itself we took to O'Connor who made an attractive base for it mounted as a coffee table. In deference to the deceased, we kept the inscription face down, unlike the present owners to whom I gave it later.

I had to go hundreds of times into the attic looking for leaks whenever we heard drips after heavy rain. Of course the tenants had never had the roof valleys properly cleaned. I also had to visit it often during the electrification of the upper flat, while George tapped with a broom to tell me exactly where I was. But it was well worth while to see lights in rooms unlit all my life. Once I fell out of it across an ancient bath, and could so easily have broken my back in the fall.

At an early stage we decided to remove a very dangerous huge beech tree in the yard. We asked in town who was best with chainsaws; it certainly had to be lopped from the top downwards. Legend had it that the family estate bell hung in it to summon workers in to lunch. But after it was felled, there was no sign of it. "Another family legend gone", chortled George. Then "ping!" the chainsaw met the bell totally encased in wood, an amazing sight. We should have left it so instead of cutting it out and selling it for £40, but at least we thereby had a profit from an awkward tree. If it had ever fallen suddenly it could easily have demolished the beautiful "laundry" building on the northwest side of the courtyard, cobbled at the sides. This Italianate stone building, elegantly designed, has a turret with a dovecote in which spectral barn owls bred in my youth, and is surmounted by a weathervane. The building was only used as a laundry in the first half of the 19th century, as we proved when George turned its ancient mangle, and out popped an envelope bearing a black penny stamp of 1841.

In the lower wing we found three floors facing the yard which had been a temporary kitchen with a horrible Rayburn cooker, a dog's room with only a small wooden box in one corner, and a room for broken furniture, had to be renewed since they were so rotten. But fortunately the very strong joists were perfect as elsewhere in the house. So we were able to renew them with off-cuts of inch chipboard fetched from the factory of Scariff at great peril in a rickety borrowed van. Large single sheets would have been much easier to fit, but more expensive. We floored the rooms for £10 after a month's work with handsaws.

Then the question of carpets. Only two were still usable, one the superb floral main drawingroom one bought in 1919 for £19, my mother used to say. It was rather faded despite the use of horrid old blinds we hurriedly banished, and underneath we found hundreds of protruding tacks and nails – why we knew not. George maintained my family had an interest in a tack factory when we even found them holding up several panels of William Morris wallpaper in the diningroom, identified as such too late, alas.

To my amazement George even know all about the qualities of carpeting. Rubber-backed ones he ruled out completely, and suggested instead good quality ones but chiefly rectangles for rooms without bays, so that they could be reversed anytime or ultimately sold if necessary. Otherwise we put down fitted carpets. In some instances, such as in our own study, he pointed out that expensive carpeting was too good to hide under furniture, so we edged the carpets with plain grey linoleum that we happened to buy at an auction very cheaply since it had been slightly damaged while being taken off a ship at Limerick docks with sharp hooks. We paid under £20 for innumerable square yards in a huge roll.

Later Youghal carpets wove specially twenty yards of 36" carpet for our main stairway, a perfect serviceable mid-green that showed off so well the thoroughly cleaned brass stair-rods. When Cushlawn carpets brought out broadloom carpeting for our lower wing flat, it could not be precisely butted, missing by about half an inch. I suggested we ignore the error in our never-ending hurry, but not he; the manager was summoned out, only to inform us we were the first people to notice the basic error. George won, and they had to take a third off the price and discount waste caused thereby.

Our initial aim was to make a small suite of rooms within the horror from which to work non-stop. But when we installed new bathrooms and toilets we found that the main sewerage system was blocked, and we did not even know in which direction to seek the ancient septic tank. After much research in the woods, we found the vast system, probably expanded in famine times, worthy of a town. It was porcelain-lined with four steps below each manhole down which I duly went in waders. The septic tank itself resembled a pharaoh's tomb with brick arching overhead, and we had to summon an excavator to straddle it and take out the contents of more than a century. Obviously inadequate use of water had let it all silt up; renewed, the overflow departed merrily under yet another field.

We never took holidays, or even an hour to go fishing initially, but worked side by side solely for each other, utterly happy, despite the awful difficulties. One day, however, we reluctantly broke our rule and accepted an invitation to tea with Ethel Hederman at Croom. Luckily we did so, since there we met a delightful couple, Mr. and Mrs. Marvin from California. He was with Bechtel Engineering, and head of construction at the nearby Gortdrum mine, and she formerly a high-powered American secretary, was his second wife. His firm had built the Intercontinental Hotel where they were staying.

After tea we chatted about our project, explaining we had only just finished three or four rooms for ourselves as a pied-à-terre. "I hate living in hotels", she exclaimed. "I must come and see your place tomorrow." Jim more soberly inquired "How will you heat it?"

She at once saw through all the horrors, and pointed out that the 'ould barn' as she christened it, could be unique, and way ahead of its time if we made three self-contained residential luxury flats for executives, being sufficiently close to Limerick. "Don't panic if one is ever empty", she advised, as one was once for a year. "Keep your rents low so that people will settle in long-term. No structural changes need disturb the lovely old place. I see it all from outside. I will give you £600 for these five rooms as an internal flat, including your new ones, and you can proceed elsewhere. We'll pay in advance if it helps. But it must be ready in two months' time".

What a push it gave us. They settled in as planned arriving with some twenty numbered tea chests travelling on company expense; these we put in the basement. "Gerry, you're in business", she chuckled amiably. We knew, too, that £600 was the rental then for any Limerick house, as an agent pointed out somewhat sourly. Boards were up everywhere for electrification, and while carrying books around she trod straight down on an ancient rusty nail that went nearly through her foot. Luckily she had had anti-tetanus injections, and I rushed her for another. (It is thirty years since they came, and I have just had another charming letter from her, now widowed.) "Boys, you are together night and day, how is it you never quarrel. I can't understand it!" But obviously she well knew, as a travelled lady, how very much we were in love.

The Marvins liked our next tenants, when we did up next the lower wing flat and let it to Jill and Jack Newman, she a former model, and he a business consultant. Thirteen pounds a week including central heating we were charging at the time, oil being still only 1/9 a gallon. (The oil tank had been very badly placed directly over our well, an excellent one and our only source of water, and one stormy night it began to leak at the control tap. I had to turn a spanner frantically and hope it would stop the leak, not put 300 gallons in our well!)

We had called in a Shell-heating engineer who drew up an extensive blueprint for the work costing it to the last pound. But George was equal to him: "That's neatly prepared", he observed, "But I wouldn't consider buying a car without knowing the horsepower. You haven't stated the BTU power of the boiler, which could be minute, as for city dwellings and utterly inefficient here!" The engineer was much surprised, and retorted: "if you're that observant, why not buy the parts and have it installed under contract". This we did, and saved quite half the quote, installing an extremely efficient system still operative today with a new boiler. Furthermore it was very neatly done despite the pipes having to pass through huge stone walls in many places.

Further tenants through the years, found by advertising executive standard fully furnished flats, minimum tenancy six months, included Barbara and Marcus McMahon, and Mrs. Bernard, a charming elderly doctor's widow who came with her own good furniture and therefore wanted a five-year lease. Michael Hickey, captain of the Irish Davis Cup team, and a former Wimbledon player, stayed a year, and twice we had engineers from the nearby Ferenka factory. Dr. Oliver head of the Thomond College had the upper wing flat for a year, and when the McMahons left, they passed on the lower wing flat to the Flynns who eventually bought the place after being our tenants for about nine years. The Flynns and McMahons both had two sons born at Thornfields – boys only anticipated.

During our struggles we made some interesting discoveries, including a first edition of Haydn's "English songs" autographed by the composer. "Come on, pa-pa Haydn, sign here, please", my ancestor may have asked the great composer, during his second visit to London in about 1795, when he would have been 18 and at Westminster school. Also thrown out in a back room was a songbook with one autographed by the librettist Da Ponte, and sheet music from Mozart's "The Clemency of Titus" which he must have admired as much as I. It was the first Mozart opera to reach London, and he was probably at its first production there. Later being a close friend of the Prime Minister Lord Melbourne, he may well have met the poet Byron who was then apparently knocking off Lady Melbourne as well as other amenable ladies. In his teens, however, Byron's closest friend was Lord Clare who lived at Mountshannon House, only a mile from Thornfields.

We also found two old gardening books, in bad repair but complete. It took George to notice they were written by William Thompson in Ipswich in 1856, the exact place and date given as the establishment of the firm, on our seed packets! We wrote to the company who replied that despite having a large botanical library they did not have these two works by their founder. One gave precise details of where he acquired all their first products; they wanted to know how much we wanted for them, and sent down a representative from Belfast to inspect them, loaded with free samples for our garden.

After protracted negotiations we sold them for £350, the most we ever received for two books, knowing there was no other buyer and that if we pushed harder they might seek the information, at least, in the British museum. The following year their seed packets showed the bearded founder reading our books.

Our best painting was discovered more strangely. We were sweeping out horrors from the basement with a yard brush when George stopped me, arm raised. "Hey, that's a canvas!" Rolled up on the floor, covered in dirt and with a small hole in it, lay an old tangled painting. Eventually, rather against my wishes, I admit, we had it framed and roughly cleaned for £11. "Norwich school" perhaps worth £150 we were wrongly told. So it hung for several years until Mealy, auctioneers, whom we were so very lucky to encounter, noticed the painting and asked could they take it to London to have it better cleaned and framed. "Not more than £100, I pleaded". Back it came after some months looking superb, and meanwhile I had found that it depicted Kilmurry Church near here, and was painted by an important Limerick artist Jeremiah Hodges Mulcahy who had a studio in Catherine street in about 1865. My family patronised his work, and about four other paintings by him were here originally.

When it came back from London beautifully restored and framed, Mealy told us: "I could get you £2,000 now for it in my auction rooms". Remembering the state in which we had first seen it, we chorused "You get it!" Eventually it made £5,200 in his auction rooms, more than twice what we received for any other picture at our auction. Not bad for a rat's dinner.

Then there was the saga of the antique stoves. We usually bought "The Daily Telegraph" when in town and one day I happened to see in the personal column an advertisement seeking old heating appliances pre. 1880. It so happened I had recently bought an "Encyclopaedia Britannica" (1955) for £50 in perfect condition, in one of Mealy's auctions, and I looked up "Nott" since we had an old free-standing cast-iron heating appliance, long-since unused prominently inscribed "Nott's Patent". To my amazement I read: "An American divine from Philadelphia . . . . . who invented the anthracite stove". So I had a complete provenance, by an extraordinary chance. I wrote to the advertiser, who was acting for the National Coal Board, and they were delighted by my discovery and sent a representative to see it. It was the oldest they were offered with a full pedigree.

At least that was so until I remembered another older heating appliance, hidden away in the basement, built into the original wall that once heated a conservatory. In the governor's "Encyclopaedia" of 1825 (5th edition) which George remembered, we found to our amazement about thirty pages on heating appliances, and the earliest they illustrated was ours. It was basically two concentric cylinders made of iron. The coal board were amazed at this extra news, and pleaded with us to take care of the pile of rust – for such it looked – and carefully extricate it with pieces of its piping complete, since they discovered that model had been made in about 1815 by Stephenson, who made the famous "Rocket Train". So it dated just after my ancestor bought Thornfields.

Now both items are fully restored in a new London museum of the Coal Board, I gather, and we were given £1,000 for the pair. (There was, it so happened, an auction of such items at Sotheby's at the time; but what if either item had not fetched its reserve, we reasoned. It would have to have been thrown in the Thames. So we agreed their sum.)

During all this time George cooked me wonderful meals, mostly in the traditional style, and rarely ruined, as he would say, with too many sauces and spices. He said he never minded all the effort since I never left a scrap. He polished carefully, made sure the lovely old clocks chimed together, dusted thoroughly and did all our laundry to perfection.

Meanwhile I would be outside digging, splitting logs, or working in the attic. Also I alone drove; he went as far as learning when we first settled in at Thornfields, but said he did not feel secure oddly enough, so he gladly gave me the job, which I preferred anyhow. Here I am in fact reminded of two elderly ladies, Miss Hetridge and Miss Jackson who owned a similar country mansion in equal disrepair near Nenagh, Co. Tipperary, when I was very young. They could only drive their old car with a joint serious effort, since their disabilities matched up; one controlled the clutch and the other lady worked the brake. Our specialities equated in a similar manner.

Understandably George found few books in our collection readable, and often took out detective novels from the library. Meanwhile I would be listening to music instead by a blazing fire of timber. Considering chainsaws far too dangerous to use, we would find someone to cut up a fallen tree, and give him half in return. Once when George was ill, I discovered a huge oak tree fallen in a most awkward position among tangled laurels and swapped it for a ton of coal delivered to our basement larder. I would be preparing half-hour-illustrated opera talks for the Irish radio, and used to drive up to Dublin to record three or four when required. In this way I gave more than a hundred, and enjoyed the work as well as access to their excellent record library, and quite good pay.

George's most brilliant decision it now transpires, came when a farmer arrived asking how much we wanted for clear title to an acre of road frontage that his father had encroached many years earlier. "We don't want £500, or so", George immediately suggested, "We want two acres back adjacent to our avenue which they took in the 'Troubles'" In this way we pushed the boundary fence right back, otherwise at this very moment people could be building houses right beside our avenue at one point. Our excellent elderly lady solicitor, Miss Tynan, fully approved George's quick decision, and efficiently arranged the transfer.

If we had been more than six miles from the city George said we could never have undertaken the huge task since it would have been too far out to attract tenants, who normally needed two cars. Also we found ourselves often driving in two or three times a day for items urgently needed for our work. Our London 'Mini' car was succeeded by a horrid "Triumph 1300" constantly needing repair, then an excellent "Alfasud" until it was written off when eight years old by a trailer coming off a passing car. I was given nothing for its loss since the driver was uninsured – as were so many at the time – but later received £1,000 for shock, from the pool covering uninsured drivers. Now I have an excellent Rover 213 these last twelve years: I have always bought lesser cars, wanting them new, not with hidden faults.

Once a visiting journalist asked if restoring Thornfields was our life's work: I replied in many ways it was. Also my good friend Ald. Jim Kemmy paid me the great compliment of giving me a civic reception while he was mayor, for my rescue of this historic place, along with my closest friend Dan Lawless, who was rightly honoured for his many years as administrator of the Belltable Theatre.

In June 1988 as part of the Irish celebrations for the Australian bi-centenary, a service of thanksgiving for the life and work of Sir Richard was given in Stradbally Church in Castleconnell, relayed by the Irish radio. The Australian ambassador Mr. Frank Milne gave an address, and I read the lesson; members of the government came down for the occasion, and afterwards I gave a luncheon at a nearby hotel. It was two years after George's death, and here was the opportunity I had sought to pay public gratitude for his wonderful support and ability that had made it possible to save the house. As I pointed out, I most certainly could not have attempted the task without constant loving support, and courage in taking on the mammoth task. Without him Thornfields would no longer exist, and the grounds would now be yet another housing estate. I would be in penury, and Thailand could never have come about.

It is terrible to recall that all this strenuous, devoted work so nearly went up in smoke, literally, on July 6th, 1992. I had been to Dublin for the day, leaving my car twenty miles away at Limerick Junction. On my return at dusk I drove up the gently curving avenue to see smoke pouring out from under all the shoots, and flames coming out of two windows in the servants' quarters over-looking the yard. No one else was at home I knew by the absence of cars. Naturally I thought the attic full of dry leaves and old birds' nests, so terribly inflammable, must already be on fire, too.

I rushed in and threw poor Susie, my boxer, but for whom I might have taken back a later train, into the car and dialled 999 for the fire brigade. I was so shocked I did not tell them it was such a very big house, and could hardly explain the way out. They told me to stay by the phone in case further instructions were required. Certainly not! I seized one of two fire extinguishers we had bought for £4 at an auction, and raced up the narrow back stairs. Black smoke was roaring away ahead of me; flames were about three feet high in two small rooms where old books, photo albums and other hoarded items lay, burning fiercely. Firstly I had had to break into the new owner's part through an intervening door.

Most fortunately the extinguisher worked immediately though only once serviced, and I doused the flames as best I could until my hair began to singe when I retreated being aware I was alone in the house. I rang 999 again, and told them if they hurried the house might yet be saved.

A fire brigade arrived after about 15 minutes, followed by two more summoned by radio when they saw the size of the place. They put a ladder in the inner yard, and rushed through the house with a large hose. They soon asked where more water might be, and I remembered the old well lay precisely under their ladder by great good fortune. Meanwhile I was frantically moving papers, videos and even light furniture out into the stables not knowing if the place could be saved. They asked whether they could take off some slates to obtain better access to the fire, and of course I agreed. I telephoned my nephews to come – the only time I summoned them in thirty years – and rang my dear friend Kit Rohan, who asked a mutual friend to dash around Limerick to try and find the new owner in whose basement the fire had evidently originated. Eventually two hours later he appeared. But for the first hour I did not know the outcome, and wondered whether my personal insurance would pay up. When the firemen told me to relax all would be well, I pleaded with them not to let all go away and they left one engine over-night in case the fire broke out again as so often happens.

About forty slates had to be taken off – since perfectly replaced – and the dear old house was saved, but if a lorry had even delayed me on my return it would have been burned to the ground. The fire had been within inches of the open attic space we later found. I was so glad George had not lived to see the drama. I claimed £250 for damage to my Dublin clothes, and very slight water damage in my part, but was sent an extra hundred since they considered my claim inadequate – but I preferred it that way, in case of a repeat performance when I am away. Strange that it had been left to me personally to save again this happy old birthplace, so long cherished by my family. "Why, it's good now for the next 200 years!" as Jim Kemmy kindly pointed out that evening at Limerick City Hall. Here now the wildlife – descendants of those I so wilfully killed in my youth – may long delight me in this last sanctuary near Limerick.

We also found a large watercolour of special historical significance though rather poorly painted, virtually thrown out. It showed Edmund Burke's home at Beaconsfield at the end of the 18th century, and although not signed, was presumably painted by the governor when he visited there during his holidays from Westminster school.

I checked with the Beaconsfield library, full provenance is so vital in these cases, and found that it did indeed show the statesman's home before it was badly damaged by fire. The well known paper company "Wiggins Teape" now owns it, and I thought they might like to acquire it for their offices. But evidently the friendship between Burke and the eighth governor of Australia meant very little to them, and they promptly returned it noting it was no way well enough painted to adorn their walls.

Incidentally it showed a flock of sheep in the foreground, and it was only when recently reading Conor Cruise-O'Brien's biography of Burke that I chanced upon the somewhat curious fact that he was a keen breeder of sheep. It was the well-known Dublin Castle genealogist, Basil O'Connell, K.M. whom I knew, who eventually worked out the exact kinship between Burke and my ancestor described at the time as 'next in the male line'. He was only a second cousin once removed, apparently, though that was then regarded as of importance. Much more so was the enduring influence of such a mentor on young Richard.

Saddest of all, however, was the theft at some stage, of three very beautiful Indian miniatures on ivory, carefully wrapped in tissue paper in a raffia box within a silver casket in the drawingroom. One depicted the Taj Mahal and the others Indian potentates. They were, I believe a wedding present from Burke's widow whom he continued to visit, and possibly dated from the time of his involvement in the impeachment of Warren Hastings.

Nothing was ever moved at Thornfields; you might have thought the furniture bracketed to the floor. For more than 160 years two local newspapers dated 1820 lay in the right hand drawer of a fine mahogany games-table, carefully folded. One was the "Limerick Chronicle". Occasionally I would read them casually, and finding no mention whatsoever of my family or home in the small print, return them to bed. Why had they been so carefully preserved?

About seven years ago I found the answer in a most curious way. The Irish television was filming an episode for a TV series "Thou Shalt Not Kill", about the true story of the Colleen Bawn. Patricia Flynn, the new owner of Thornfields, happened to be a friend of the series producer, a son of Cyril Cusack, and it was arranged that the filming for the 45-minute production would almost all be done at our house and grounds, since it resembled closely the mansion, 25 miles away, Ballycahane, down the Shannon estuary, where the Colleen's murderer John Scanlan lived.

I then remembered that those ancient newspapers had reports of a trial of a certain Scanlan for the murder of a 16 year old girl in that area, but alas had sold them shortly before. They described the trial of a 'squireen' officer, who had arranged a mock wedding with the girl whom he fancied briefly, before taking her on a pretended honeymoon down the Shannon where he had her murdered as soon as his infatuation waned. By an extraordinary chance the producer asked me to play the part of Justice Richard Jebb, who tried the case in Limerick courthouse condemning Scanlan to death, without knowing that it was my great-uncle's father I would impersonate!

The gallows on which our Scanlan was hung was erected in our walled garden, and a tavern and a shoemaker's shop were both assembled in our ample basement. A make-up studio was arranged overhead my flat. I was carefully decked out in a large white wig, and red-and-white attire, although the actual scene was only shown in a black-and-white flashback. Thus I made my sole stage appearance, much to my surprise, and managed my fiery 40 words aimed at the accused, despite my lack of memory for lines.

While working so hard on the house, we occasionally paused to arrange the sale of some item to help defray out heavy costs, having determined never to borrow from a bank. "At least we'll own what we manage to restore", George had long maintained. Before we met the excellent Irish auctioneers, Mealy Bros. of Castlecomer, Co. Kilkenny, this usually meant taking it to Sotheby's or Christie's on our very rare visits to London, usually in turn, for a few days.

Perhaps because of my legal background I am a keen reader of small print, the finer it is the more suspicious I become. In this way, in a dull moment one evening by a big log fire, I found at the bottom of the back page of a Christie's catalogue the statement "Vendors overseas 10%, not 12 1/2", in about 1968, after I had sold some paintings there for about £2,000.

I wrote pointing out that Ireland was overseas from Britain, especially since a republic, as much so as Belgium, and further. I suggested a refund of £50 was therefore due. My letter was very poorly received, almost rudely, after a long delay. They said I was the first person to raise the matter and therefore, by implication, wrong. Stung by this I wrote about a month later suggesting they sent me fuller sales rules if such there be. This only brought forth a photostat of the same back page!

Meanwhile I had asked a friend at the Irish Embassy in London what the position should be; he only replied evasively that it depended on the circumstances. The £50 sounds very small today, but at the time it was sufficient to wallpaper about five rooms – we always preferred it to paint, our ancient walls scarcely ever being good enough.

On we struggled until, like our boxer dog with a rag, I tugged again; I visited a Limerick solicitor I had never engaged before, it so happened. "Oh, I only deal in property, and livestock sales", he observed casually. "In that case I'll dictate the letter", I suggested. It worked: back by return came the £50, and an apology. Obviously it was not the minute sum involved that caused the difficulty, but they did not want me to set a precedent. He was amused at the outcome, and charged us only ten shillings, perhaps because he knew his elderly sister had been our regular solicitor in her retirement, having only kept on some convents, and 'the boys'. One year her Christmas present for us had been our joint Will – how vital Wills are for gays. Oddly enough she had never before encountered a client who chose to leave legacies as fractions of the estate, that seemed only logical to us, and included pages of examples to our amusement; she was known as Ireland's most meticulous lady solicitor.

At about that time we went to a local auction of the contents of the home of a great-aunt of mine who had also chosen to settle near Castleconnell in her old age. Georgina had caught my bachelor great-uncle Edmund, who usually lived at Kingstown Yacht club, when he was about seventy and had lost his resolve. Her husband had been killed in the first world war. Shortly before her death aged about 90, not over a bridge table as she had hoped, she tried to persuade me to turn Catholic, and when I refused promptly docked the hundred pounds I had been told to expect.

Anyhow we liked the old lady and visited her often. Over the entrance to her drawingroom had been screwed two very old dark oak altar pieces that we used to admire, as best we could from underneath. She paid scant attention to them, and we were never told their history. Nobody bothered to take them down for the auction, attended by the usual covey of dealers. We decided to bid to £17, and trust our judgement. When we were overtaken by a dealer, however, George put in a quick small jump to £25, and down came the hammer.

We helped unscrew our purchase, and they stood on our hall table for about four years; each was about six inches square, and they depicted the resurrection from the tomb, and a tranquil nativity scene with cattle peering down. There they remained until George happened to go to London, and knowing he would stay at a small hotel near the Victoria and Albert Museum, he placed the carvings in his case as an afterthought.

Next day he visited their department for assessment, though not valuation, of items brought in by the public. His small parcel created quite a stir. "These appear to be 16th century Flemish altar pieces; you should really take them to the Rijksmuseum in Amsterdam for examination". This being impractical, and costly, he instead summoned a taxi: "Christie's, please."

But on arrival he was rapidly deflated when their examiner announced "Oak, religious, little demand for those, you know. You might get £40 for the pair". And George had told him about his visit to the V & A.

Luckily he had time to walk across the park, a scene he loved so well, in the sunshine, to Sotheby's auctioneers in Old Bond Street, distrusting the abrupt dismissal he had received. After he had waited a while watching visitors unwrap their treasure, a young lady looked at his carvings and exclaimed – as did Marguerite on seeing the casket of jewels given her in "Faust" – "Can they be real?"

She took them backstage, and after a very anxious wait

George was told by a senior examiner, that they were indeed 16th century Flemish. "How would £600 - £800 seem? I will advise you about reserves at a later date". Naturally he rang me excitedly with the news. "I had a gin and tonic, and did not notice it", said the usually moderate drinker. "So I had another!" A London QC friend of ours said he often dined out on the story, warning friends to make sure to check values at more than one house; obviously any can make similar bad valuations at times. But this one had been spot on and we received £750 after commission.

It is unfortunate when one learns things just too late in life. We scarcely knew what pamphlets were until we saw some early examples fetching very high prices at a book auction. Then we understood why a visiting solicitor book-collector had quickly given us £13 not long before, for a fat leather-bound volume just marked "pamphlets" that we had not had time to examine. Later we realised it probably contained a collection relevant to Edmund Burke, and would have been of great value. We made few bad mistakes over all, I hope, but this was probably one of them.

One more brief example of the chaos that confronted us in the empty rooms of the wing. As a boy I used to play with a rather battered pistol with a wooden handle, a mid-19th century Dutch seaman's in fact, though I certainly did not know that at the time. We found it among so much debris – in two different rooms; there had in fact been a pair, but I had never before seen them side-by-side. I think they later fetched about £50. A cased pair of duelling pistols would have been a better find; but as George always said: "Gerard, be content with what we have discovered". As indeed we were.

One day a visitor interrupted our incessant blowlamping with a very large blue folio under his arm. It was John Sheehan, a neighbour from Castleconnell, then unknown to us but soon to become a very good friend, with his wife Fabyan, and little sons Ross and Conor – the "weather forecast", as George called them.

"I don't know where to begin!" he exclaimed, unwrapping a 25 page genealogical tree, with extra pages for other family branches, and illustrations of various knights in armour. "Here is your family pedigree back to the 12th century", he stated to my amazement. Bourkes in abundance – or De Burgo in the most distant past.

It transpired that John's mother was a Bourke, too, of a different branch, hence perhaps this vast labour of love prepared in his spare time, showing again how people excel at work unrelated to their livelihood. (Just as a friend of mine, Desmond Meikle, a law student in TCD with whom I used to tour the university botanical gardens for a lecture thereon, later became director of the Herbarium at Kew, his law joyfully abandoned.)

We were astonished at the elaborate tree, and it soon became obvious that he was no-way disappointed to find it would end abruptly with me. My bachelor status had clearly blown it over. Once in Sydney when asked about this, I replied truthfully that marriage was one thing I was not prepared to contemplate merely for the purpose of lineage, and therefore live a lie.

The tree began with Adelm de Burgo, who married the daughter Agnes of Louis VII of France, the pater-familia of all the Bourkes. Then more specifically comes William Fitzadelm de Burgo, who married Isabel daughter of Richard Coeur de Lion, and settled in Castleconnell in 1199, having apparently been viceroy of Ireland in AD. 1177.

Later my branch came down through the third viscount Mayo, the same cheetah crest and 'A Cruce Salus' motto, who turned Protestant in 1726, and is also apparently a forebear of our former president, Mary Robinson, née Bourke.

When the 7th Lord Castleconnell died in 1697, the succession was vested in Lord Brittas, who sat in the Irish Parliament in 1689 before going into exile. Later the 5th Lord Brittas and 10th Lord Castleconnell died unmarried, but a brother Thomas Bourke was a general in the Sardinian army, a strange occupation, before dying in 1788.

John explained I could in fact claim still the double title – "What good would THAT do?" chirped George, correctly. I was later persuaded, nevertheless, to send the extraordinary tome to the College of Heralds in London, which replied after a year that although it was a brilliant collation, the titles had been attainted in 1691. John still insists I could acquire them by a different route – but so what. Their Pretender I remain.

Groups of Australian genealogists call at Thornfields sometimes to see the governor's home and vault marked: "Sir Richard Bourke and his descendants", though it has not, in fact, been used this century. One day, after much persuasion, we opened it – with the only key out of about 30 that we had found labelled – and saw inside, his coffin draped in purple, bordered with silver, looking completely undecayed. Six other family members keep him company in death, including two very small coffins of grandchildren. We laid flowers, prayed and closed the vault.

But what an amusing sequel this had in Sydney some years later. I went to an evening of gay-related films at Glebe, and from another coffee table a voice called over: "Hello Gerard! I've been to your home, when you kindly showed us around your family church and explained the tablets, and later gave us coffee in your flat". Then, he added bluntly, "The group was very surprised to find someone so 'out' in the wilds of Ireland, and wondered, as we left, whether you had restored the place for your family or your lover?"

Chapter ten

The Spring of 1986

I am amazed how vividly my memories of long ago have appeared while writing these recollections, such as Billy's smile across the college chapel 60 years ago, and I now approach the central chapter with trepidation. I replace just one veil of privacy least I am unduly saddened while I write of these most tragic months.

When I first met George he surprised me by declaring that he never wanted to become old. "You can be old, if you like, but not me, I hope!" I think it was because he had seen too often the implications of poverty and old age in his young days in London. Anyhow when we began work on Thornfields we were both fit and even chanced having no medical insurance for the first few years, until we joined the Voluntary Health Insurance as soon as we could afford it.

George had been warned when about thirty that he should smoke less since he had a rigid chest formation that Dr. Holmes told him would certainly cause him difficulties in later life. But he continued to smoke about ten cigarettes a day, inhaling too, whereas I just played around with two or three and never inhaled.

About six years after we returned to Ireland George first began to suffer from asthma. I returned from Dublin one evening to find him holding onto the sink while cooking, and for about a year he used to wheeze occasionally in his sleep. I sometime wonder whether the terrible asthma that quickly followed was partly caused by blowlamping all that old lead paint in confined spaces, or whether he was often too close to our boxer Tim, whom he loved so much. The first two years Tim would sit on George's lap in the mini-car with his big head out the window, but his hairs must have blown straight back down George's throat. Also he loved him so much he let him sleep on his bed for a while: "One turn, all turn!" poor George laughed, ignoring the dangers.

The doctors gave him no comprehensive allergy tests to try and trace the cause of the illness that gradually overtook him and was so terrible to watch. A rapacious chemist even let us pay large amounts for medication, not pointing out – until we changed shops – that George would certainly qualify for a medical card. When he inherited £8,000 from a friend, as did I, he insisted on calling to the medical card people to inform them of his changed position. They were amazed at his honesty, declaring they could not recall anyone acting similarly, and pointed out the income from the money would in no way affect his entitlement.

One winter George became so bad despite the fact we left on thermostatically controlled heaters at night, that I was allowed to give him 1/2cc. adrenalin injections that helped him breathe initially. I hated injecting him on the shoulder, where he soon resembled a pincushion; but the advantage faded after a few months and his condition deteriorated alarmingly.

One awful night in 1975 he was on the floor desperately trying to breathe, and when I rang our very inefficient country doctor to ask if I could give him an extra injection he replied sharply: "No, you cannot. You can do no more", he told me roundly. Luckily I had the presence of mind to reply: "In that case I want the ambulance." "Oh, do you?" he answered rather angrily. "I'll have one sent out." (Asthma is one illness with which you can officially admit yourself to hospital since speed is often essential in a life-threatening attack.)

This was I think the second time I had to call an ambulance; George told me he was always glad no bells rang on the return route. They had told him there would be oxygen in it that would help, but it failed completely to do so. When I arrived in an hour later, as usual, I was told the chilling news: "He is not responding to treatment." Naturally I was aghast, and bereft. Apparently when Dr. Nash then head of the hospital, and an asthma specialist luckily, had seen him he told his staff "Intensive care at once" since he could not even lie down he was so badly caught for air.

I went in twice daily, at least, to take him things; but he looked terribly ill. One moment I thought he was going – and turned away to hide my tears. He took all the medications without any fuss, only asking to be told what the various items were for, reasonably enough. If they hurt him, he would just say, "I know you are not doing it for pleasure.!" He was kept in intensive care for two weeks, and then returned to the private room I always had for him, thanks partly to VHI. Dr. Nash brought him a message there one day, to his surprise, "The nurses in ICU want me to tell you that you were one of the best, most co-operative patients ever, and wish you well" That from the normally fierce Dr. Nash – whose gentle hobby was making violins.

When George came back from the hospital early in 1975, I soon became very unwell, and our doctor told George I only had nerves because he had been so very ill, and prescribed me ninety tranquillisers a month! The chemist even asked George who could have been prescribed so many. He hated giving them to me naturally; but after a few days mercifully, our ignorant doctor was away – and fortunately for his patients dropped dead at a medical conference – and George had the opportunity to call out of retirement old Dr. Dwyer who immediately diagnosed me with emergency prostate trouble. The other one had not even given me a rectal examination, especially since I was only 53.

Next day I collapsed for a week having refused to go to hospital unless to a private room, uncharacteristically. For that awful time George, unwell himself, had to nurse me, assisted at times by Kit Rohan, not being able to drive.

A neighbour drove us to the hospital – me complaining about the springing in her car, I was in such pain – when the room was ready. George even had to push me in in a wheelchair.

After an examination by their excellent specialist Mr. O'Donal, who asked me who I had for a doctor who let me become so ill, whereas I could have been operated on about two years earlier,I lay there in comfort on automatic flow, and drinking litres of milk, for a month before he dared to operate, telling me he had once operated on a similar problem too soon and encountered extra trouble. Mercifully George had not mentioned the possibility of cancer to me – but they inquired my age almost daily. Everyone nearby was in his seventies.

As I waited on a tray for my four-hour operation, a young nurse said: "Gerard are you anxious?" "No, should I be?" I queried. To the anaesthetist asking would I prefer a local anaesthetic I just shouted "No thank you!" Anyhow the operation was a wonderful success, done from behind – it even worked again about a month later when we ventured in that direction. And all the young hospital nurses had been so charming I did not turn away: I became so used to them fiddling and examining, they had to say: "Now Gerard you can pull up the bedclothes, and be more modest if you wish". They'd met a naturist!

All that took place ten years before my George died on April 9th 1986. He had reflected how easily we could have both gone ten years earlier. Although the final decade was so difficult for him in his medical condition, our love never wavered for an instant. "Good luck if you meet someone else", he finally remarked generously. "It won't be for another 42 years!"

Two years before his death he woke in the middle of the night, a day or two after asking me to make sure all our emergency telephone numbers were at hand, and was unable to move his left-hand side. He apparently had suffered a stroke, though mercifully his speech and face were no way impaired. So I had to phone dear Dr. Margaret Callaghan in his presence to tell her so; naturally she rushed out at once, and the ambulance was summoned again.

What a cruel blow this was, added to all his great discomfort from years of asthma, always guarding against sudden temperature changes, and trying to make sure no dust or other allergens existed. In hospital he struggled daily to overcome the ghastly stroke, explaining he wanted to be a little better every time I saw him; otherwise he would not have bothered to try.

The nurses held him up as a model patient to those similarly afflicted. I still went twice to see him most days, and towards the end often three times, since we had a rota of private nurses, and I had to cover the 8:30 to 10:30 am period myself. "Gerard, you'll soon be a SRN", they would quip. (After his death, I asked the night-nurse whether it was the first gay relationship she had nursed. She told me: "Yes, and I have been most impressed. Gerard, it is now your function to tell uncertain young men that if they have a fraction of your luck, they too can lead really happy confident gay lives". Which is partly the purpose of this book.)

But now I see unsummoned the approach one night late of a young lady doctor who, almost trembling, told me that George's mind had gone. I almost fainted: but instead walked over softly and talked of things he knew and loved, and back it came before sadly I withdrew . . .

George was in a wheelchair for a time, but gradually recovered all but the use of his left hand. I helped him to have about thirty sessions of physiotherapy with blind Mr. St. George, who always sensed my extra presence. Then came the day to take George to Carrigoran Nursing Home to recuperate for about two months, in the very efficient nicely-run home twelve miles from Limerick. I would have my own lunch there, excellent it was, while helping George to cut up his, chatting to two English ladies at our table, who told us no such facilities were available in their country at the same charge. It was run by a very caring Order of nuns. George shared a double-room with an elderly farmer – who to his horror had never heard of Johann Strauss – who always offered to go for a stroll when I called. Better still his doctor soon gave me permission to come and take him out, not for a drink as suggested, but for comforting privacy and love.

It was about then that our tenants approached us about wanting to buy Thornfields, saying they had looked everywhere, but could not find a place they liked so much, which we took as a friendly compliment.

Since it would be difficult to sell items they wanted to keep for the house, prior to auction, I had to ask Mealy's auctioneers to do a full valuation of everything in the place. Meanwhile George's condition had worsened again, alas, and he was back in a private room in Limerick Regional Hospital. He endured the most awful series of tests for my sake, he explained. I tried to be with him at the time naturally.

He was 66 by then – we never celebrated birthdays, or gave presents, regarding our lives purely as a solid unit. Then to my great dismay Dr. Peirce told me alone in mid-March that poor George "had no future"; he had met me on the stairs, and had evidently explained also to him that but a month or two remained. I bore up as best I could though down more than a stone in weight never being able to go for walks in case I missed a phone call. He said he knew I had an auction to attend to in early April, and would send George home two days after it was tidied up.

We had always imagined there would be an auction at Thornfields one day of our excess possessions, and hoped we would attend it together, having done so much research into the things we both liked so well. But alas it was not to be. George asked how the auction had gone before it actually took place, and I did not have the final satisfaction of telling him how excellently it went, thanks in many cases to his own astute buying at auctions, through the years, and our restoration of so many important pieces.

The auctioneers arranged to have the avenue patrolled by police nightly after they had added much extra property into the sale; we were ultimately only selling about 250 lots, only a half-day's auctioneering, after what the new owners had bought by private treaty, so much outside property had to be added. But the auctioneers explained that by adding items of similar or better value they would thereby attract dealers from far and wide. They erected a marquee on the lawns with closed circuit TV so that people who had not been able to come to the viewing knew which item was being offered. For me they arranged speakers in my drawingroom so that I could keep the tot, fortified by coffee, or drinks, brought by Kit. Later she told me the devout Mealy brothers, we both knew and liked for some years, had knelt down and prayed for the success of the auction, the first they had given in the west of Ireland, from which they very worthily derived more business I was glad to hear.

I had put high reserves, as I thought, on my favourite forty items, thinking I would receive enough without selling everything – fortunately George had lived long enough to choose what items we excluded from the auction for our ground-floor wing flat. In the event only one item, the lovely oil painting of my great-great-grandmother Ann Wise of Cork, aged about eight, painted in about 1805 by Martin Archer Shee P.R.A. was the only item that did not reach my reserve; how suitable, since it was always George's favourite painting that we hoped to have properly cleaned one day. Unfortunately he was too ill to be able to explain to him that things he had bought for tenners were now making hundreds in several instances, he had such an excellent eye for antiques. I did not wait to hear the books being sold, since it was time to see him again.

Oh, God bless him, in many ways he had grown more attached to our possessions than I, and had lovingly looked after everything carefully through the years. Also once on the antiques road show they explained that if you have no descendants to appreciate such pieces they are better sold, since those who pay good money for works of art respect them properly.

Kit had cooked for about ten people, auctioneering staff, in my kitchen, with Michael gladly at hand. They had already promised George that they would always look after me, when he told them so sincerely that the only thing he minded about dying was what would become of me. "You have no-one but your sister", he had told me. "That is a bill I now have to pay", I replied. "I have never regretted for an hour living so very closely for each other without intruders".

As arranged by Dr. Peirce, George was sent back two days after the auction. A nurse settled him in what is now my spare room where we had twin beds. I was given a huge supply of medication for him, and there was talk of a district nurse coming to help me at times – but I felt I would never need her. Since one evening as I left Carrigoran at dusk I was suddenly told to tell him: "Don't worry I'll see you out of this awful situation". I thought how extraordinary, how will I ever be able to fulfil my promise. "Oh, rest in the Lord, wait patiently on him", as they sing in that lovely Mendelssohn aria.

I believe in predestination, as well as in reincarnation, now I am Buddhist as well as Protestant. Only now did I discover why on my arrival in London I had been so very keen to learn the whole text of Elgar's masterpiece "The Dream of Gerontius" oratorio with the wonderfully consoling words by Cardinal Newman, as Gerontius leaves this world and passes gently to the next. "Jesu Maria I am near to death, and Thou are calling me . . . that sooner I may rise and go above . . . Go forth upon thy journey Christian soul . . ."

As my darling George lay dying this music was constantly in my mind; only those who know it well can fully appreciate its extraordinary worth in that situation. Later Brahms' "A German Requiem" composed for those who mourn came to mind as well. Afterwards I could not face hearing them for more than a year, their purpose fulfilled.

Kit and Michael were with me much of the time, making sure I fed myself. He could hardly take any nourishment, but at least he did not suffer the indignity of incontinence. On April 9th they stayed longer than planned since they rightly judged the end was near. In late afternoon I came out alone to tell them George had gently left me in my arms, just as we both would have wished it to be.

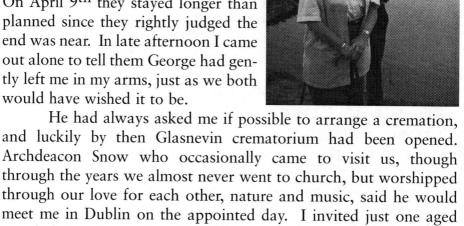

He had always asked me if possible to arrange a cremation, and luckily by then Glasnevin crematorium had been opened. Archdeacon Snow who occasionally came to visit us, though through the years we almost never went to church, but worshipped through our love for each other, nature and music, said he would meet me in Dublin on the appointed day. I invited just one aged couple living there whom we liked, to form a quorum. Then to a perfect farewell. Brian Snow just said a prayer for George and a prayer for me. We had met alone and departed so, after 42 years of mutual adoration.

While George was trying to recover from the stroke we used to go shopping early and buy a few items daily, thereby giving him the chance to walk safely with my assistance. It so happened a young friend in one of our regular shops noticed us on our daily passage. "Good morning!" his lovely deep voice would call out, great beauty adorning his smiling face. "How is your friend today?", if George paused outside while I bought the item.

Later he read about the auction, and soon afterwards I went in most sadly to tell him my friend had gone; it was daffodil time, and I had taken a bunch to Glasnevin much wilted en route, not that that mattered at all. So seeing he had several lady assistants in his shop, when he said "You two must have had a lovely place", I replied, "Why not come out and pick daffodils with your wife, if you like sometime", and walked away unanswered. I doubted the offer would be taken up, but naturally wished for such charming company.

Apparently he had been told we were gay; gossip spreads quickly, not that I have ever minded it so applied. So two weeks later he very kindly called out, not with a non-existent wife, but with a nice young friend from Dublin also about twenty years old. I was delighted to spot them from the kitchen summoning up courage to call in. How we then laughed and chatted happily once our secrets were revealed. They were naturally surprised to hear I had had such a glorious long love affair, and I hoped theirs might start now in similar intensity. Here, too, was exactly the crutch I needed to try and start my life again.

He very kindly came out alone about four or five more times, and we chatted and had drinks. I tried to explain it is no-way wrong to be gay; one has to play the hand of cards one has been dealt. So I greatly enjoyed these visits of an hour or two, feeling we might be able to help each other in important ways. He looked so very beautiful, kind, but sad; naturally he told me about his family, and how close he was to his dear oldest sister, a year his junior. But he added how anxious he was that his Dublin friend might not be true to him – the inherent anxiety of youth – and after the third visit told me that he was suffering badly from depression, to my horror. I was arranging to drive him out for some treatment the following week.

Then on Friday the doorbell rang and I rushed to open it for him, but there instead stood his sister in tears. I absolutely screamed when she told me he had died tragically – it was by far the worst shock of my life, especially since I was already very weakened by George's death. How could the crutch be kicked so cruelly from my arm? The full effect of this news I cannot here express. But his dear sister told me she would always try to take his place, a wonderful remark, kept fully to this very day, as a loving tribute to her brother.

The old adage states it is darkest before the dawn, and so it was to be. She kindly coaxed me into town to join her friends for a drink. "My good friend Dan Lawless will be there, you'll love him, he's outrageous." How lucky I was not discouraged by the remark; like the gay comedian Dave Dale said: "Outrageous I may be . . . but only half the time.", and that is the right proportion.

In this way I met my closest friend Dan, the perfect combination of complete sincerity, kindness, ability, and so many more excellent facets to his character. Everyone in Limerick knows and admires Dan not only for his former work as administrator of the city's "Belltable Theatre" – I saw him act superbly once in Pinter's "The Hothouse" – but for his innumerable kindnesses to people in so many strata of life, gay or straight. Now, too, I happily place beside him in my remarks, his close friend Clive, who are together making a lovely house high up on the hills behind Thornfields.

It was not many days I am sure until I first met his dear mother Nancy, too, then both running the city's best known flower shop, so efficiently and happily. Her chief attribute is love, she exudes it, and it was no wonder Na immediately christened her "Mama Nancy" when he stayed here, and that she is now the devoted Godmother to our daughter, Sirilac. What a difference their friendship and that of their family, including father Pat with his triumph in circumnavigating the world alone on his third attempt, has made to my life since George's death. In reality, and in utter sincerity, I feel adopted by them all.

To spare their blushes, I cease the list of the accomplishments except to admire particularly Nancy's excellent oil paintings now coming to full fruition in her retirement, and her generosity in lavishing such care on her annual summer garden party that supports almost entirely the city's vital gay switchboard system. It was their wish that I should complete these memoirs that would never have proceeded otherwise. Nancy's comment: "Gerard, you owe it to life!" finally won me over.

Her seaside holiday home near Dingle where I have spent cherished days, has that unsurpassed view of the Blasket Islands as in the film "Ryan's Daughter". In this Gaeltacht area she is fluent in Irish, and there surely admired also as a 'wise woman' a seer and confidante, whereas I alas know not my Irish voice.

After George's death, when I suddenly had too much time, I decided to try and combat loneliness by seeking further provenance for some of the best things we had withheld from auction. Foremost among these was a beautiful silver-gilt wine jug of 1867 engraved with Grecian figures, and a handle comprising a serpent climbing high to reach a small butterfly landed upon the lid. It bore the inscription: "To Richard Bourke from his grateful ward Charles William Wise".

No family records mentioned my great-grandfather's ward, and I often wondered who he might be. In records of burials I eventually discovered that two Wise males were buried near Cahir, Co. Tipperary in 1879 and 1880, but nothing else.

So I decided to visit Cahir, about 30 miles away, on a hot summer's day to see what I could find. And what an amazing day ensued. I asked in a general store whether they knew of any Wise family in the area; after some discussion among themselves, they told me they thought an elderly lady living alone about five miles away had been born a Wise, and now lives at Rochestown House.

At the end of a long avenue I was greeted by greyhounds barking fiercely, but inside I met elderly Mrs. McClintock excitedly watching a race meeting on television. I let her continue this important task before stating my case. "Yes", she said, "Charles William Wise was my grandfather, I can even show you his fishing record books for 1875 if you like. He loved to fish the nearby River Suir with his young son to whom he was so devoted. They had many very good catches there".

Then her face darkened. "A most terrible thing happened. The boy Billy, then 14, jumped down awkwardly from a high wall and a few days later died from peritonitis. His father, only 42 years old, went to bed and turned his face to the wall in total grief. Six months later he was dead". I had listened in silence, horrified.

"Perhaps you would like to see their graves", she continued, regaining her composure, "they are buried in Ardfinnane Protestant Churchyard, in the top right hand corner, if I remember rightly". I thanked her for relating the story of our family ward, and off I went. Ultimately I found the graves where she had indicated, very overgrown; as the last furtive rays of sunlight lit the patch, I saw them side by side, together in death. The boy's grave was simply inscribed "Blessed are the pure in heart for they shall see God". But his father's inscription was so appropriate "Blessed are they who mourn for they shall be comforted". I shed a tear for them, and George; surely a predestined day?

Chapter eleven

Australia

In our young days George never stood in the way of my travelling alone on the continent for music. Only once when I suddenly thought of trying to go overland to India did he express such alarm at the inherent danger that I cancelled the idea forthwith. But he used to remark, while we toiled restoring Thornfields, how much I must miss my early travels abroad. To this I replied that no one has everything in life, and I lacked nothing having him.

So when during his last dreadful illness bulletins began to arrive detailing plans for the 1988 Australian Bicentenary I stacked them away in a bottom drawer, wondering whether I might indeed travel there one day. Might it not fill an endless void, when seemingly I must soon walk alone?

In the event, nine months after George's death, I began planning the first of five annual visits to Australia pouring over large-scale maps of Sydney. I studied the Potts Point area, south of the Opera House on the Bennelong promontory named after Governor Phillips' young pet aborigine kept on display in such a very unseemly manner. But phone calls to guesthouses in the area, an easy walk across the park in daytime to the Opera house, past Farm Cove and the Botanical Gardens, proved unsuccessful.

Our close friend Aileen Thackeray's niece, Rosemary, one of her two beneficiaries, lives in the fashionable north shore Mosman area, and I wrote to her seeking advice. She kindly offered to put me up for a few days while I sought suitable accommodation for my two months' stay, but warned hotels in that area might well cost £100 per night.

On the way out I broke my Quantas flight for four days in Singapore staying at the famous Raffles Hotel, then still in colonial grandeur before its recent updating, especially since agents were offering a special rate of four nights for £100. On arrival I even found myself the proud user of the Nöel Coward suite with a foyer of rattan couches doubtless often filled by a carefully chosen few. For he was among many writers, including Somerset Maugham, who chose this eastern refuge. So where better to experience the exciting Orient for the first time?

The drive in from Changi airport is remarkable only for great lines of exotic fan palms where still exists the infamous Japanese POW camp of that name. But the superb hotel proved an ideal oasis for me still not strong after George's death. I only ventured out on a short harbour cruise to see Chinese junks weave between modern shipping, all so different from anything I had previously encountered. Being almost on the equator, the hotel is everywhere embellished with massed orchids and at breakfast – a splendidly comprehensive help-yourself – singing birds enchant you from cages placed aloft.

In one smoking area, tiger footprints were copied to represent the poor beast said to have been shot by sahibs in the famous tiffin room. At the long-bar I tried their special gin-slings more notable for their expense it seemed, than their coveted secret ingredients.

I scarcely ventured out, however, since supermarkets and other stores seemed all to be encased like formidable gasometers, so fearful are the Singaporeans that signs may defile the city that may soon become the first to prohibit smoking in public. No, there was enough for me to admire within the safety of Raffles Hotel, even my first monsoon downpour that suddenly crashed upon me, and the remarkable oriental beauty all around. But alas when I finished my first dinner there alone in style and realised I had just consumed crayfish and cassata, two of George's favourite dishes in his absence, loneliness hit me hard.

At Rosemary Dean's highly prized home, merely because from it one can glimpse the harbour setting, I saw a magnificent oil painting of Queen Victoria reviewing troops in Phoenix park, Dublin, by the great British painter Fernley sen. that I had last seen in her mother's diningroom at Aldershot.

Their daughter Annabelle, then about 26, was a prominent writer with the Sydney Morning Herald, and oddly enough was delegated to interview me soon after my arrival. The paper, founded during Sir Richard's administration was critical of his liberal ways, as she admitted in the piece for which I was photographed in front

146

of the elegant statue of my ancestor. The effect was ruined, however, when they rudely insisted I remove the jacket of my suit to look more Australian.

My hosts declared they would make no attempt to show me Sydney, but instead let me off with a sketchy map of the main streets as my guide, adequate since the centre is, in fact, surprisingly compact, and very easy to explore. I took one of the frequent ferry boats to Circular Quay, the wonderful central mooring where not only ferries tie up, but also cruise liners, even including the Queen Elisabeth that fits the main berth exactly. Then where to go first was my problem, to look for accommodation or to see places of such importance to my background that I felt they might disappear unless I hurried.

Outside the Mitchell Library, the state library of New South Wales, stands the statue of Sir Richard by E.H. Baily, erected in 1842 by public subscription, and considered one of Sydney's finest. On it I found inscribed some two hundred words of tribute to him and his accomplishments, that frankly made me blush. Later within the library I found many prints of Sydney in his time and bought a selection for Thornfields. On hearing who sought them they made a special effort to find extra ones especially some made from paintings by Conrad  Martens, the great water-colourist whom he patronised.

The lady director, Barbara Berzins, visited Thornfields shortly before our auction, having been alerted by the Australian ambassador that items of importance to them might be available. When she saw the important set of five miniatures on ivory of the governor at the time of his engagement in one frame with his fiancée, his father and mother, and only sister, she said they were essential for her library to hang in the director's office just behind the statue, so I agreed she might buy them in advance by private treaty.

Later she and members of her staff took me to lunch, an occasion slightly marred, however, when a staff member told me the governor was also much admired for his administration as Lieutenant-governor of the Eastern Provinces of the Cape from 1827/28 and that I should consider visiting Johannesburg. I replied that a person known for his compassion, even before his term in Sydney would most certainly not approve my visiting a country enduring apartheid. There the matter dropped; it was doubtless on account of the way he handled the Hottentot minority problem that enabled him to behave correctly with the Aborigines.

I then walked up Macquarie Street to see the Legislative Assembly which he partly founded, the only parliament building, I understand, freely open to the public. I happened to telephone the secretary of the Australian-Ireland Society just before they were invited to dinner there, and they kindly invited me to join them – as a prime exhibit, I rather felt.

Later during my stay, the N.S.W. premier Barry Unsworth invited me along, and after a chat about my ancestor, kindly took me into the chamber much to my surprise; they were discussing workmens' compensation, but he stopped the deliberations and told them the descendant of their founder was among them. I was generously greeted and stayed there a while out of courtesy. It was indeed lucky I had read Dr. Hazel King's excellent biography of Sir Richard before I left, and in consequence knew more about him than merely my relationship. (It was published by O.U.P. Melbourne in 1971.)

Next I decided to visit the Opera House and celebrate my arrival with a good lunch on its smart terrace. Many exciting musical evenings were to follow there through the years. But unfortunately though designs by the famous Danish architect Utzon have formed a magnificent piece of sculpture the building is very unsatisfactory for opera. The reason is chiefly that the opera auditorium had to become the splendid concert hall and vice versa when a new government complained halfway through the belated construction that some part of it must quickly be completed. It has resulted in the opera orchestra pit being far too small, as is the stage itself, and operas requiring large instrumental forces cannot be accommodated and have to be given in semi-staged performances in the concert hall instead. Until recently only about 75 players could be fitted into the orchestra pit, and are there deafened and cramped under the stage. "You cannot expect hi-fi from a telephone kiosk", one player commented wryly.

The same day I walked up Bridge Street in the company of family ghosts. For there in December 1831 on their arrival after four wretched months at sea, my poor great-great-grandmother, Betsy, a heavy lady in her fifties, must often have walked that hill to the Botanical Gardens being, like her husband, very keen on botany. For there in Bridge Street stood their new home, First Government House, the town residence unlike the more spacious Parramatta Government House, some 15 miles out of town, approached up the Parramatta River on a route recently revived.

Luckily my search for accommodation ended when I found the "Jackson Hotel" at Potts Point. It was a terrace house well done up in the Victorian style of about 1880, as I felt well qualified to judge. When the proprietor found I was related to an early governor, being historically aware, he agreed to lease me a pleasant double room at about £20 per night. It was at the good end of Victoria Street leading from the infamous King's Cross sex-trade area, a moral hazard by night. (Once I saw there a man sitting on the ground hand-cuffed around a tree, and hurried by . . . another time a guy called out, as I waited to cross the street: "Your turn now dear!") The street was furthermore, lined with old banger cars which had taken groups of backpackers across vast Australian terrain and were now up for sale, hopefully at a profit, to equally daring adventurers.

I had only been at the "Jackson" a few days when I met Chris Ryan, about 25, working as a room boy. I correctly judged him to be a nice friendly guy to whom I could express my loneliness since

George's death. At once he responded beautifully by inviting me to join him and his Tamil friend, Herb, that evening to see a film. For he had once been a nurse, and had even in his youth had the awesome task of nursing his young lover dying of leukaemia. So began a very enjoyable close friendship that lasted through my Australian visits, and later I had the pleasure of entertaining them at Thornfields for a week. Chris was a leading dancer and choreographer with the "Sydney Dance Front", and on my last evening I had the difficult choice of seeing him dance nude, or going to dinner with the speaker of the Legislative Assembly. The first option won.

Very soon after my arrival in Sydney I contacted Ray Thomsen, one of the closest friends of George and I before we left London, whom I had known for some 35 years. He had worked at Australia House and in the travel business, and was certainly our cleverest and most widely travelled friend. He is also unsurpassed as a wit, and raconteur, and has a photographic memory. Indeed he was short-listed once for Mastermind answering on the great art collections of Europe, since he knows where almost every picture hangs, and its history. But in the event he had to return to Sydney before the final test to look after his aged mother, being moved into a nursing home. He is equally knowledgeable on music, and will reel off the cast of an opera we both attended, unknown to each other, in the early fifties. I retort "Wait a minute Ray, I probably could not afford a programme that night."

George and I played bridge with him in London too and I felt he gave me a special warm welcome out of deference to my loss. Being as keen on tennis as I, he introduced me to two Johns, in their late sixties, one of whom was a representative for Dunlops, who kindly gave me tickets for the NSW Open Tournament where I could again watch great players in action.

The Johns had a lovely suburban home where I occasionally visited until the tragic sudden death of the younger just after returning from a holiday in Thailand, a country he also admired. They had even met Na at the Hilton in Bangkok, inviting us to lunch to admire the hotel's superb gardens where much photography took place, with Na as the chief target.

150

Ray called me 'walking history', and introduced me to friends of his interested in early Australian history, notably Gordon and Brönte who lived up the Blue Mountains near Bullaburra in a charming wooded area frequented by parrots of every hue. There we enjoyed a spectacular 'fête champêtre' for Brönte's 60th birthday, and once stayed as guests. Alas both are now dead.

They took us on several historic drives up the Blue Mountains and were eager to show me places where the governor and his "gay entourage", according to contemporary accounts, explored and his courthouse at a site nearby. Surveyor Mitchell did much expansion up there at the behest of Sir Richard who was himself always anxious to see the progress of such work unlike some of the other stay-at-home early governors who apparently were more interested in wenching than exploration.

Berri Groome, exactly my age, who formerly worked as a reader on the "Sydney Morning Herald" but took early retirement, bought himself a small house in the very much wanted Paddington district of Sydney, at the end of the long Oxford Street – how anglicised the names. Beautiful wrought-iron balconies embellish the houses there, now much sought after, though rather cramped within. There he sits reading from a large library, chiefly paperbacks, but with some autographed volumes by the famous Australian laureat writer Patrick White, to whose works he introduced me.

I stayed twice with Berri as a paying guest, and he also gave me several introductions, whereas he mostly sat reading alone with classical music playing loudly.

Sometimes I brought back Asian friends: one day when I lunched at a pub nearby the young manager had evidently noticed the company I chose. He served me with beef, with rice or vegetables. "With <u>rice</u>, I presume" he declared roundly – Australians have a habit of declaring those who choose Asian friends "Rice Queens." But he then came over and apologised saying he had a Malaysian friend – I showed him photos of Na – and found his clientele made frequent racist remarks, especially the cricket and rugby fraternity.

When at the "Jackson" I wanted to go swimming and Chris suggested 'Boy Charlton' swimming pool nearby, but not as pleasant as the open sea, to my mind. Ray had, of course, already taken me to Manly Beach on my arrival, but there huge dumper waves can be a bit too violent for the aged, as is the strong undertow. One tourist was rescued there three times on the same day I once read to my horror. The sea-pool looked dirty, so I determined to find a more congenial place to swim.

It so happened a nice-looking bronzed guest at the "Jackson" returned from a swim one Sunday, and I thought where he goes so must I. He vaguely said he had been down to Watson's Bay. When I explored the area soon afterwards I first encountered 'Camp Cove' and thought it might possibly be where he chose to swim. But no, a little further on over a rocky path, with many wild flowers such as blue columbine in flower, I met "Lady Jane" - a character in "Patience" – more correctly dubbed Lady Bay, an inlet nearest the southern Sydney heads at the entrance to the harbour. A notice read "Nude swimming beyond this point only". So I had at last found a secluded place exactly to my taste; hopefully one's sunglasses would filter out the five-per-cent female form.

At the time there was a high rickety ladder only, giving access to the nicely curved beach keeping out the less intrepid, but in later years it was replaced by handsome new steps. It lies below an Australian Naval Base, and is scarcely overlooked; it is tidal, with limits of about 20 feet, and only when the tide is fully in is one forced up against the overhanging cliffs. There were no shark-nets; one just had to hope a shark passing into the inner harbour did not fancy your spinner. It has scarcely any shade, but some rocky areas could be reached at low tide, on the right, with caves in which happenings were rumoured to take place. I thought age precluded such explorations; also voyeurs sometimes stationed themselves above. No, Lady Jane's main beach was quite enough for me, and very enjoyable.

Such a relaxing place. Down you go, position a towel, and off with your clothes – unless you are Asiatic in which case you seem to go down to observe others, while strictly concealing your own contents, rather to the annoyance of the regulars. You could take a picnic lunch. I once grandly took a half lobster salad ; otherwise a little boat would come in every two or three hours with sandwiches and soft drinks, and ice-cream. A dog onboard barked loudly as the boat was beached, unused to seeing a queue, naked as you please.

A certain camaraderie existed there; people were friendly and well enough behaved. On one of my early visits there I was much surprised when a guy about 40 said from the next towel: "But I've met you. You're Ray's friend, he works at our theatre "Her Majesty's", but failed to introduce you to me, while he did to my friend the manager, Don."

That was how I met Tony Magri, who once played football for Malta, my 'malteser' as George would have named him, who subsequently became one of my best friends in Sydney. He and Don held smart annual garden parties to which they always invited me, chiefly for theatre folk, and Don sometimes took me to the Opera, since Tony was not so musical. It had been he, oddly enough, who had handed me my press seats at Covent Garden many years earlier.

I also met Bruce Fone there, where he used to sun himself for hours seemingly fearless of melanoma. His old New Zealand friend Harald, once a well-known ballet dancer, sometimes accompanied him. One year I asked Bruce to try and find me a room near his flat, up from Bondi Beach, in lieu of Berri's place. Being unable to do so, he invited me to be a paying guest in his own large flat where I had a happy stay waiting for my Thai house to be completed, two months later. "You don't act like an old man, why dress like one?" he asked one day, dressing me up in bright colours – soon I noticed my contemporaries there similarly styled.

He was also about 40 and half English, but had been very wild in his youth; he had a pleasant group of younger friends who often came to barbecues on our veranda. On Saturdays I would shop with him and choose some more classical CDs for his collection. The Christmas was enlivened, too, by the presence of the wife of a bishop from New Zealand and one of their sons, Bruce's latest acquisition. She was escaping an angry home-life since his Lordship had not spoken to her for several years.

It was great to have Bondi Beach easily accessible – it was

before the recent craze there for nude surfing – and sometimes bring back takeaway suppers. Strangely I once met a philosopher there, who had written in four-foot high letters right round the sea wall: "You have not loved who never have forgiven". But, alas, before I left Bruce, who had a good job as an accountant, was stricken with very high fevers. Often I went searching for medication at night. Not long afterwards he spoke of going to live up near Cairns in some gay retreat he knew; I did not enquire too deeply since I knew he was already being tested for HIV and was in the 'grey area', being counselled before I left. Alas I heard no more . . .

Sydney was a wonderful place in which to live out my delight in sharp contrasts. I could relax swimming soon after paying a courtesy call on the governor of NSW. The director of the Mitchell Library arranged the visit shortly after my arrival. The press officer told me to bring my camera; until then I did not know that the full-length painting of Sir Richard in uniform that had hung on the stairs at Thornfields when I was very young, had ended up suitably in Government House.

My ancestor ordered the present government house from London architects as First Government House, now the site of Sydney's important new museum, was becoming dilapidated, even rat-ridden, he wrote before his departure in 1837.

The Governor kindly showed me over his beautiful demesne at the edge of the botanical gardens, after I had waited at security on my way in, and he greeted me over coffee. He showed me the impressive portrait, and where our crest is carved among those of other early governors on the castellation of the building. It was not actually finished until two years after my family departed. Occasional chamber concerts are given there, now the new governor has relinquished the place to the public and lives modestly in the suburbs, perhaps in preparation for a republic?

Among the first invitations I had was one from Caroline Fairfax, a member of the millionaire family that owned the "Sydney Morning Herald" until quite recently. It was for a family Sunday luncheon at "Bellevue" their aptly name residence on a promontory overlooking the harbour, and considered one of Sydney's most splendid homes. She later showed me their fine art collection including many Conrad Martens paintings in which I am much interested.

A prominent member of the board of Old Government House at Parramatta, Caroline arranged my first visit there, a most exciting day for me to see come alive the name I had so long known only from the Castleconnell church tablet to my great-great-grandmother. The house situated high in an open park, is looked after by the 'friends of Parramatta House', who escort visitors around. The porch was certainly  familiar since my ancestor copied it as an addition to Thornfields on his return.

We went out in the Fairfax's shooting-break with three other guests. On arrival I was not allowed in by the back entrance, but led in formally, somewhat to my surprise, by the main door and invited to sign the gilded VIP visitors' book. The curators were also alerted about their unusual visitor, and their chief expert on Australian furniture was also at hand, who had once called at Thornfields some years earlier.

The rooms are carefully arranged in mid-19th century style with memorabilia from the early governors displayed. In one were portraits of the first ten governors, and I was photographed beside my eighth, to whom they thought I bore a striking resemblance. But I was aware, to myself, how cramped Sir Richard must have felt after his more spacious rooms at Thornfields.

A case of stuffed birds I passed in the corridor, noting it failed to include a Bourke parrot; in another room were examples of porcelain from dinner services used by some of the governors, none as nice as the two Meissen butterfly 1825 plates I am leaving to the museum in due course. Sir Richard had a vast service made for his sojourns in South Africa and Australia, some of which, much broken, I inherited. "Why are the butterflies different this holiday?" I used to inquire. Obviously because others were smashed and replacements taken from the unlocked store.

After our picnic, we walked across to the graveyard of St. John's Cathedral to see the grave of my great-great-grandmother. The inscription on the flat limestone slab had long since eroded away. I had no opportunity to buy flowers to place there, but laid some wild flowers carefully instead. She would have understood they came as from Thornfields with my love and admiration.

She lies, oddly enough, within the same grave railings as Lady Fitzroy, wife of the next governor, who was killed along with her aide-de-camp when her trap ran away down a hill and struck a tree. A plaque denotes the spot. I have been back there four times since to see my family's country home for six years, during which my great-aunt Anne acted hostess for her father, and his second son Richard was his personal secretary when 20 years old. It was there, too, that Anne once sang a song recital accompanied by William Wallace from Waterford, composer of "Maritana", who went to Australia as a young man. "She sang very prettily", I have read. Furthermore her father gave him 100 sheep for having enjoyed his music so much. (Incidentally Anne, who was born in 1806, lived on in Sydney until 1884).

Once I had lunch near there at the "General Bourke", and the new owner asked if I knew anything about him: curious he had never bothered to inquire at the museum half a mile away. But my finest memory of Parramatta is of reading the lesson in St. John's at the lectern beside a beautiful memorial to dear Betsy, with inspiring words from her grieving husband:

"Reader, she was the most gentle and affectionate of God's creatures, correct in all her duties; she led a life of unassuming virtue and practical piety. She was the comfort and solace of her husband, the friend, teacher and nurse of her children, and a blessing to the poor. He who places this marble to her memory would indeed be the most wretched of mankind, did he not feel the Christian's hope of meeting in a better world her who he has lost in this".

The most important invitation I received that year was to Admiralty House, the Sydney residence of the governor-general, Sir Ninian Stephen. The invitation was for 4:30 so I anticipated a garden party, and was surprised to see no cars when I arrived. I waited a while, and then asked was it not 4:30. "Oh, yes, you're expected soon", they replied; so I was escorted up past magnificent floral displays to where I was welcomed by Lady Stephen, and soon joined by Sir Ninian for a homely tea.

He was a lawyer, once considered as a mediator for the Irish talks, and knew all about my ancestor's legal innovations, and various changes at the time. He pointed out, too, that my ancestor was not only one of their most important, and certainly most compassionate, governors, but had to act directly in those days in view of the inevitable delay in seeking advice from London. When I mentioned I was going to Melbourne soon afterwards, he advised me to visit its La Trobe museum to see important papers of the period.

He then showed me the state dining room and our two fine crested silver-plated candelabra, two wine coolers and four candlesticks, dated about 1825 by Matthew Boulton one of the best silversmiths of his day, which the Australian government bought at my auction. At least they have ended up in the ideal place, looking out to the Opera House, and I told the butler softly that it was now his job, not mine, carefully to clean each piece. Sir Ninian said they were very pleased to acquire them to grace the governor-general's table for ever more.

The following evening he had invited me to dinner at Government House in Canberra, a great occasion. I was telephoned and asked would I be able to accept if invited, as is customary. I quickly confirmed my acceptance and the inherent honour to my ancestor, ignoring the fact I was supposed to be setting off on a four-day visit to the town of Bourke in central NSW a few days later.

Oddly enough the people there, a very backward largely sheep shearing town on the Darling River, that frequently dries up, have a thriving historical society and had long been sending me their annual reports, and had asked permission to use my crest. So I partly felt I should make the visit, six hours by train, even though Sir Richard never went there, and they chose his name for some obscure reason. My Sydney friends were horrified that I should think of inflicting such a roasting on myself merely to see my name spread around the town.

But when I wrote to the doctor with whom I was due to stay and explained I could not refuse the Canberra invitation, it fell on very stony ground, and I heard no more. So Bourke remains unseen, and it is "Back o' Bourke" as the saying goes, denoting the limits of habitation. (I still recall my surprise at Aravon seeing my name writ large in the middle of NSW on my atlas.) Incidentally Queen Elizabeth went there in March 2000, hopefully aware it was named after one who represented the British crown in Australia so many years earlier.

So off I went to Grace Bros. to hire evening wear to take with me on my bus journey to Canberra, comfortable and cheap, for essential long distance travel. I stayed at a good hotel, and dressed with special care.

We were asked for 7 o'clock. After passing through minimum security at the end of the beautiful wooded approach avenue, I was welcomed again by Sir Ninian and Lady Stephen and thanked them for their honour in inviting me alone the previous day. The dinner was for 43; I had been sent a placing list in advance with details of those to be present. We were seated at one very long table, their Excellencies central, opposite each other. I was given an elderly lady, Mrs. Chaney, to escort in procession; some ambassadors were present, and the Hon. Rose Talbot de Malahide, and the director of the Sydney Opera were there for me to meet.

The sumptuous dinner menu I give for those interested: coquilles St. Jacques au gingembre (wine: Hardy's Keppock Gewurztraminer 1980). Sorbet de Pamplemousse. Supreme de dindonneau au miel et thym. (wine: Petaluma 1979 Coonawarra). Pêche au champagne. At the end Sir Ninian rose to drink a loyal toast to Her Majesty the Queen, which he followed greatly to my surprise by adding "For Mr. Bourke, the President of Ireland". I suppose I must have been the only guest not owing allegiance to the Queen.

In the drawing room afterwards I chatted to the director of the Australian Opera, telling him how much I was enjoying my visits to his company, and of Sir Richard's great love of music, which I have inherited. Later I wrote an article for their magazine about his musical interests, connecting it to Mozart's opera "La Clemenza di Tito" which was then being staged in Sydney. At about 11 o'clock the dinner party ended, and the cars were called.

I returned once to Canberra to stay a few days with a former Ambassador to Ireland, Sir Peter Lawlor. He showed me round the fine new city built for the next century it seems out of the constant rivalry between Sydney and Melbourne with both considering themselves the true capital for various reasons.

Be that as it may, I saw there fine examples of new Australian architecture including the High Court in which, as Sir Ninian had pointed out, the courts sit in the Irish manner so many of its judiciary being from there over the years. I was also shown the Canberra National Library which bought three of our four Conrad Martens paintings at the Christie's auction in 1965.

These they brought out carefully preserved from light in special folders, and I noticed the one of Lapstone Bridge which Christie's had failed to have cleaned from foxing at the Courtauld Institute was now fully restored. I ordered good copies of them for Thornfields. The huge new Australian Federal Parliament building was then only about half finished, but I could see it looming at the end of Anzac Way. At a special luncheon, too, Sir Peter had invited their chief historian Prof. Manning Clarke to meet me. It seemed odd chatting to the old gentleman who knew so very much more about my family than I do.

The only other city I felt bound to see was Melbourne, founded by Sir Richard, and so named in March 1837 after he had received permission from Lord Melbourne, Queen Victoria's prime minister, to name it in his honour. "You can call it after me", he replied. "Nobody will ever hear anything of it". So was born the great new settlement.

As the plane flew in over Melbourne I was naturally very excited. Below I saw the ultimate planned city, not the original plans which my maternal grandmother so foolishly threw out for paper scrap from her rented home in 1914 after the death of her only son, Gerard, killed in action. Would I be able to erase all buildings, even skyscrapers, from my sight, including those on Bourke Street and see the area the governor had surveyed with Hoddle planning streets as wide as O'Connell Street in Dublin? (How very odd that some years later I happened to talk to Hoddle's great great grandson when he stopped to admire my boxer dog in Limerick). Together they "traced the general outline of a township upon a beautiful and convenient site".

I thought, too, of my ancestor's great bravery leaving Thornfields in August 1831 to take up such a distant appointment with his family. In fact the voyage from the Canaries lasted about four months – we found daughter Anne's diary of the trip – often in horrific storms, with Betsy frequently extremely ill. Her husband, not a good seafarer himself, read prayers on board at dusk each day. Possibly the great strain hastened her death four months later, arriving in Sydney's hottest weather. I stayed near the excellent Victorian Arts Centre that includes the opera house, concert hall and art gallery, alongside the Yarra River. It was originally called the "Yarra-Yarra" when Sir Richard explored it, calling it "a fine limpid stream, the most beautiful I have seen in all New South Wales". From rivalry, Sydney wags now call it "the only river with the bottom on the top", seeing its present polluted state.

A journalist called to interview me for "The Age". "I'm not taking you to a particularly smart luncheon", he observed, "But I think it will amuse you". It certainly did at the "Bourke County" with RB beaming down from overhead the bar, and out directly at me from the table-mats that showed him planning the Melbourne streets. For the article I was photographed walking up the main street, Bourke Street, the second being Elizabeth Street named lovingly for his Betsy.

When I called as advised at the La Trobe museum, the curator showed me the slender diary Sir Richard kept in March 1837 while exploring the Yarra, and founding the great city. Until March 23rd it referred to the future city of . . . . . then appeared the name

"Melbourne" permission having presumably arrived from London. Curious indeed that I just happened to walk up Bourke Street for the first time on the 150th anniversary of its naming!

I thought it might be a nice gesture to call also on the governor of Victoria at their government house near the botanical gardens. But when I telephoned his secretary I was curtly told I could come down and sign the visitors' book if I wished, despite having told him my connections with the city; furthermore the governor was then Irish. Instead I spent a pleasant morning in the gardens seeing my first black swan remembered only from some early Australian stamps I once owned.

When I came to the small La Trobe cottage museum I mentioned to the old assistant my background, and he said its director was Irish and might like to meet me. Then on the phone he actually said to me: "Yes, I am republican Irish from Connemara", adding some remark in Gaelic for good measure. I put down the phone and reflected how rude, and nationalistic, the Irish abroad can sometimes be. (In his book "The Irish in Australia" Patrick O'Farrell is so concerned with the various Catholic bishops of Melbourne he has space – or consideration – for Sir Richard only in about five lines of oblique references.)

Those two rude rebuffs were the only ones I met in Australia. In Melbourne I sought out firstly a charming nun whom my dear friend Patricia Vasey, an Australian former lecturer in law at Queen's University, Belfast, advised me to see. It so happened that she too had been recently bereaved and we had together a sympathetic, consoling luncheon.

Patricia had sent me a wonderful letter to Sydney listing four or five people she would like me to meet while staying in her home city. The list included a pair of solicitors "fortunately not encumbered with children" who took me for an enjoyable drive up the Hawkesbury River, and her dear school-friend June Bärtl whose home I visited several times in a northern suburb, sometimes to give chats to her lively music group at their monthly soirées. Patricia had carefully given me details of the friends mentioned, adding, to my delight, "I hope I have not been defamatory to any of the above."

Ray also put me in touch with two Melbourne friends, long living together, who took me for drives, firstly up the Dandenongs, a hill overlooking Melbourne, like a garden of exotic ferns, and other luxuriant foliage where the lyrebird still dwells discreetly. Another day we toured the Mornington Peninsular stopping it so happened, I discovered later, at exactly the spot where Sir Richard stepped ashore from H.M.S. Rattlesnake.

While there I met also Lady Mabel Tate, once a well-known actress, who invited me to a performance of Britten's "Peter Grimes" by the Australian Opera, and lunch in her Tate restaurant, named in her honour since she gave it some hundred important theatrical costume designs beautifully framed. She married one of the Tate brothers, prominent in Limerick business early this century, after whom the Tate clock is named, and told me much about my own city, to my shame.

I planned my 10-day visit to Melbourne around a season of opera being given by the Australian Opera as guests of the Victorian State Opera, and went nightly to opera in one of the finest opera houses I ever saw. It has learned from the errors of the older Sydney Opera, and in addition to a huge sumptuous red-and-gold foyer with elaborate restaurants, it has an orchestra pit that would accommodate about 150 musicians, and the stage is very wide and splendid technically. I also saw there "La Traviata", and a recent Australian Opera "Voss" based on a novel by Patrick White, with music by Richard Meale. Some Australians insist it is a finer work than "Peter Grimes", an opinion with which I certainly would not agree.

It is said that Melbourne is more staid than Sydney, more English perhaps, and has often three seasons in a day, as even my ancestor suggested in his diary, I was amused to see.

Back in Sydney, a lady asked me whether I had visited SCEG-GS (Sydney Church of England Girls' Grammar School). I told her I had not deemed it essential viewing, until she explained it was in fact an extended version of Barham House, the first home of the governor's daughter Anne and her husband, Colonial Secretary Edward Deas Thomson. Their famous architect Verge built it in

1840 for all of £85. I found it was right in the centre of Sydney now, just off William Street, whereas my print of it in 1845 shows it then surrounded by extensive gardens and lawns.

Their lady archivist could hardly believe who had knocked on their door, and loaded me with statistics of the fine house the Deas Thomsons owned until about 1870. "Your great-aunt had 13 children here", she mused, making up for my later generation perhaps. And there I saw a formal staircase copied from memory by Anne from the one at Thornfields, I reckoned.

I often encountered lasses from SCEGGS again on Sundays at St. Peter's church just outside their grounds. There I found a very congenial congregation in one of Sydney's ten Bourke Streets. The attendance, about 50% gay I reckoned, also included people ostracised from other churches for various reasons, including alcoholics, or drop-outs from the King's Cross area, as well as lawyers. A true spiritual communion of some 65 souls. I often read the lesson since they seemed to enjoy a non-Australian voice for a change. Dogs were welcome too, like the big ridgeback retriever that used to sit near my pew with his master, mourning their lover who had died of AIDS.

At Christmas they had candlelight processions and a charming crib. One evening as I prayed there for my George, the vicar put an arm on my shoulder and whispered "Don't worry Gerard, there are many here in your particular position". Later he kindly invited me to lunch. Alas St. Peter's is now no more, I hear, since the land it occupied has become too valuable, and commerce has won a protracted battle.

What of the city's famous "Mardi Gras" procession held with such enthusiasm at the end of February by the gays of Sydney, and screened around the world? All the city gives way for the evening, and cheers it on, as about 40 floats decorated in outlandish manner sweep by with gays in wild abandon, leading off to the racecourse where a party for about 15,000 then takes place to general delight among the younger folk. The floats were often amusing, including "Adam and Steve" showing two lads embracing clad only in G-strings, "Dykes on Bikes", "Canberra Fruits", "Gay Airline

Stewards", and "Asian Friends" I did not miss! But next day the party is over . . . and one could be chased in Oxford Street until one found a house marked "safe haven", or thrown over a cliff by gay-bashers. Sydney is no-way as tolerant as many imagine, utterly unlike Thailand.

Once when I watched it in heavy rain, I stood near a group of young Chinese and one, Canny, 28, invited me to share his umbrella. We chatted a while, since he spoke reasonably good English. He had escaped from Canton – I never found out exactly how – where he had been manager of an electrical firm. His grandfather had been killed and their property taken by the new régime. Two of his partners had been arrested. He explained he was now in Sydney studying English, and asked would I help him with it.

It later transpired, during very pleasant swimming expeditions, and meals in Chinatown, that the group had had no idea what kind of a parade they had been watching. He could not believe all the participants were gay, and when I explained I was also, he declared I was the first he had met! "In China we are expected to marry before the age of thirty and furthermore be seen sleeping with our wives, and one child is usually the maximum allowed". I told him China must, in fact, have the same ten per cent as other countries even so hidden underground, quoting the Kinsey report, and there we let the subject rest.

I was disgusted to find that poor Canny, whom I grew to like much platonically, had to pay out about £2,000 every year to renew his visa by joining yet another English course; the teachers and curriculum varied almost every term. Later I took him to several special immigration departments to try and obtain refugee status for him. But how was he supposed to have documentary evidence of political persecution? One evening he cried during dinner, explaining he had in reality no option but to commit suicide or go underground. At one time he was delivering pizzas in a broken old car at high speed to try and earn extra money – he who had played in the Bach double violin concerto when about nine, and knew Einstein's theory of relativity when 17!

One idyllic Christmas morning I spent fishing in the harbour with him and two other young Chinese friends. Another day he drove me up the Blue Mountains with his girl friend, also Chinese, who later deserted him just as he had a little flat prepared for themselves. She just disappeared totally, a most despicable act. The last I heard, long ago, he was driving taxis in Sydney having presumably gone underground in despair, therefore being ineligible for any benefits. At least I had learned something about Chinese food during our long friendship, though I never mastered chopsticks. Together at Taronga Zoo, he would exclaim "We eat that in China!" at almost every exhibit, to my surprise.

It is known as "the zoo with a view", looking down towards the Opera House and the harbour bridge. When I first took a ferry across to explore it alone I asked the office "Is there really a Bourke parrot?" "Certainly, sir, aviary number 13". And a staff member accompanied me to see me greet a family emblem. It is also known as the pink-bellied parrot, or the night blue-winged parrot, still wild in southern Australia, and named in honour of Sir Richard. (An ornithologist in London on hearing I was off to Australia inquired whether I knew of such a bird). Nancy's son Jim once bought me kindly a T-shirt in Bahrain, made in Thailand, showing a pair of the lovely birds – it was the only one in the shop, too. At Taronga I lunched suitable enough in the Beastro, Australians like to employ such witty names, like my florist "The Itchy Palm"

There are many islands within Sydney harbour. I was once advised to see a small one, "Goat Island". There a young Egyptian student welcomed the sole visitor that morning, and was most surprised to hear I was a descendant of their history. She showed me the stone ammunition store built at the Governor's suggestion, bearing his name aloft, and explained how the island was also used as a quarantine place for newly arrived convicts. I saw their terrible night abodes, like slightly enlarged dog kennels. Other stone buildings were roofed with slates so similar to those at Thornfields I felt they must have also been Killaloe slates brought out as ballast. She showed me also a long rocky seat by the shore which still bore wear from convicts such as Boney Anderson, who was chained there for more than a year for some crime born of terror, until his screams were so intense people beyond at Balmain complained. She also had other items relating to my ancestor in her small museum.

Among the many strange items we found discarded at Thornfields George noticed a photo of a mansion set in woodlands entitled "Elizabeth Bay House" in very good condition, very old and nicely framed. It was marked "Platinotype, framed at 203 George Street". We thought little of it at the time. But I found it was the famous large later residence in Sydney of Edward Deas Thomson, my great-uncle. No photographers now exist at that street number, but at the Mitchell Library I learned that they were there from 1884-8. They told me such a photograph would fetch more than £250, especially of such a well-known house.

It now stands with only a small well-kept lawn and garden; long gone are the depicted trees and shrubbery. An oil painting of him hung inside the door, and I explored the 1860 style recreated interior. Then I showed the curator my photograph, which pleased him greatly, since it was older than any they had and in much better condition. They gladly paid the £250: I explained it would go towards my annual commuting, at the time, to Sydney. In Ireland it might have fetched a fiver.

My father's only brother Ulick Lancelot, four years his junior, studied medicine and after my father inherited Thornfields, left for Australia where he became a popular doctor in Newcastle, north of Sydney. Unfortunately, however, there had been some dispute over family silver, as so often happens, and my father did not hear from him again until shortly before he died, though they had apparently been happy friends in their youth. The severance hurt my father deeply. This is now forgotten, I am glad to say, and soon after my arrival in Sydney I met Hope Merewether, then very elderly and nearly blind, alas, who had been very good to Uncle Ulick after his wife left him.

She had written to me at Thornfields after his death in 1961, the same year as my mother, asking me if I would please add his name to the new tablet I was preparing for Stradbally Church, which of course I was pleased to do.

I was delighted to meet my "de facto" aunt at her lovely flat

166

overlooking Double Bay. She was still a wealthy hostess, living as in the 1920's, a founder member of the "Queen's Club" where she invited me several times, and once held a farewell cocktail party for me before I left for Ireland. She was a subscriber to the Sydney Opera and concert societies, being very musical, and often invited me to accompany her there. Afterwards we would go to the Intercontinental Hotel where she would conclude by asking the pianist, whom she knew well to please play Schubert's "To music", to end our happy evening together. Her son, Richard, had studied the French horn at the Conservatory, once the governor's stables.

She also took me to an exhibition at the gallery of aboriginal art chiefly, run by Ulick's grandson Anthony "Ace" Bourke whom I met briefly. When George and I were first working on Thornfields he once stayed a night and regaled us with a strange story of how he was living in Chelsea with a friend- and a young lion bought at Harrod's!

Recently he has mounted an important exhibition at the new "Museum on the site of First Government House" called "Flesh + Blood, a Sydney story 1788-1998". His mother is descended from Governor King, so who better to tell the fascinating story of Sydney family histories interconnected as strongly as ours. Furthermore I was delighted to see the important prominence he gave to the fundamental position of aborigines in any Australian story

While in Sydney I also went to the Landsdown bridge at Liverpool opened in 1835 by our ancestor as the state's first stone bridge, and bearing a plaque in his honour. Afterwards there was a celebration at Government House, and Conrad Martens

was commissioned to paint the lovely picture of it we found at Thornfields, signed and dated, now in the Canberra National Library. Another stone bridge he opened I had more difficulty finding at Lapstone, near Richmond on the way up the Blue Mountains, until I went there with Canny and his girl-friend for an outing very un-Chinese.

I also made a trip down to Botany Bay, not far south of Sydney and still quite tranquil. There Captain Cook first landed on Australian soil in May 1770 from "The Endeavour" and immediately claimed the land for the British crown though, as John Molony points out in his recent "History of Australia", he ignored the fact that he had been ordered to do so only with the consent of the natives. This he certainly did not obtain – there is a small memorial to those who were killed by the intruders – and merely because they were not using the land, he felt justified in taking it. Did he actually expect to find them cultivating the point of his arrival? I wonder how much my ancestor knew of this dubious confrontation.

Australia Day, January 26th 1988, the actual bicentenary of Governor Phillips' arrival in Sydney was a great occasion to see. I arrived about a month early and called at the centenary office to ask whether I might be given a seat among the thousand or so elect to be placed in front of the Opera House for the ceremonies. I was told abruptly that they had long been allocated, but felt it might not anyhow be wise to be trapped there long hours in January's heat.

On the actual morning my first thought was to go off swimming if I could escape the flow of humanity streaming, most amiably, towards the Opera House and Farm Cove, from early hours. But then I changed my mind, and decided to be sociable and join in their flag-waving elation. People scampered along by the botanic gardens, doing little damage. Nobody among the enormous crowd carried drink externally or internally – alcoholic that is – as far as I could see all day.

Ultimately I staked claim to an elevated square-yard looking exactly across to the Opera House with the great bridge behind it, ideal for photography, shaded by some large Moreton Bay fig trees. I noted with pleasure, too, that fate had placed me almost beside the

"Abo" tent, their centre for the day. I felt my ancestor had worked that one out.

Among the wonderful array of great sailing ships arriving from all parts of the world, was the "Asgaard" from Ireland, carried part way I learned aboard a larger craft. I thought to pay it a visit where it was berthed in Darling harbour one evening at about seven o'clock, explaining my Australian connection. But when I saw a reception was already taking place, hosted by Mrs. Haughey I was told, and guests were already being sick over the side, not from any motion, I decided it was not necessary to appear.

Some years later I thought of possibly retiring to live in one of Sydney's "Anglican retirement villages", and the vicar of "St. Peter's" showed me over his pleasant but tiny flat in one such place. He explained that tenants were interviewed aged over 68and if accepted after stating their financial positions and other personal details, they then paid a lifetime payment of about £30,000, and would be looked after for the rest of their lives, having initially done one's own work while able to do so. There was also a maintenance charge of about £1,000 annually.

Oddly enough it seemed a reasonable proposition at the time, though dear Nancy was horrified at the prospect of me 'diminishing myself" by making such an unnecessary move. I was partly drawn, I think, by my love of the sea, availability there of a good musical scene, and also excellent FM classical radio which was not then available in Ireland. One could have a guest to stay for up to a month, but consider the inmates' horror if Na, my young Thai friend, had come to stay. Also how terrible it would have been to be surrounded by people many of whom did not have the good fortune to be as well as I.

I went for the interview and was accepted as honorary Australian for the purpose. Curiously enough I did not consider the inherent pitfalls of sorrow and loneliness inevitable in a big city; in London I had always been so shielded and supported by George's love and that of his dear mother.

For about a year I was on their list for the next available flat a t Glebe. But when news came of a vacancy and I wrote to the

Australian Embassy in Dublin for my residency permit that I had always been led to believe, even by the governor-general, would easily be forthcoming – it was when the infamous Brian Burke had just left as ambassador to face trial back in Perth – the First Secretary answered in his absence. I had explained fully about my ancestor when applying and my restoration of his home. Nevertheless I was abruptly told of a new rule whereby anyone over 55, with not relations there, must take with them about £250,000 to obtain residency.

Luckily I had meanwhile met an Australian businessman in Thailand who, hearing I was thinking of settling in Sydney, warned me to check carefully my tax position before making such a move. He had to live outside his homeland for tax purposes, he explained, and considered their system one of the world's worst.

So I wrote to the Dublin Embassy and told them they could keep their residency and I would do a U-turn with my life and instead build a house in north Thailand near Chiangmai for my long-time Thai friend and his family. The secretary then replied he happened to know Chiangmai, and what an idyllic place "if only it wasn't so hot". Later when Ambassador McCarthy was installed he wrote that he was 'shocked and saddened' at the rebuff, and offered to have my case specially reviewed. But I again told them to keep it, since it had brought me to my senses, and made me make one of the best decisions of my life, choosing Thailand instead.

Sorting out the last remnants of the governor's tableware that I inherited, I noticed that an attractive set of about 20 pieces of silver—not the biblical thirty – could be assembled each with our crest, and dated clearly from the time of his administration. Forks, spoons, cruets, a butter knife, and salt spoons I grouped together as a nice representative collection. I took them out to Sydney and sent them on to a silver auction planned for Bourke Street in Melbourne with a reserve of about £2,500. I had never seen examples of crested silver from the other governors' tables on display. However, my reserve was not quite reached; Australians prefer to spend money on houses and yachts rather than antiques, I was told, since they are more easily seen.

But the following year, on my last visit to Sydney, I thought to offer them instead to the Historic Houses Trust telling them they had failed to sell in Melbourne, as they were already planning the "Museum on the site of First Government House".

I explained I had been rejected for Sydney residency and was therefore gladly building myself a home in Thailand for myself and Na. If they gave me £2,000 cash for these items it would nicely cover essential household items when I returned up there shortly. There was a slight currency control on at the time, though I now have full permission to send as much as I like to my Thai daughter.

After much deliberation the directors agreed my terms since I told them otherwise I was putting the silver into a Sydney auction two weeks later. I now reflect on my success while watching Thai television on a very good receiver, and taking items from an equally smart fridge. George and the governor would have much approved this exchange I feel.

Before closing this chapter, I recall a strange Sydney encounter of musical interest at about this time. It happened at a street crossing; a tall blond young man stood by me. "Where are you from?", he inquired casually. When I courteously responded, he answered: "Oh I'm from Sweden, and my name is Björling". "Any relation of the great pre-war tenor, Jussi Björling?" I asked. "Why yes, I'm his grandson", he answered smiling. "I'm here to give a recital in the Town Hall tomorrow night. Why not come along". I did so, and was treated to a close copy of just what his grandfather might have given at his age. His elegant family tenor, of very similar timbre, provided an evening of much pleasure, and brought to mind his grandfather's magical singing on pre-war recordings.

I close the Australian chapter by quoting Dr. Hazel King's account of my ancestor's departure in 1837:

"On the day of his departure, so many gentlemen attended his levée at Government House that it took an hour for them to file past and make their farewell bows. The opposition press expressed amazement at the number of 'respectable' persons who attended. With the scenes on the foreshores and on the harbour, however it was disgusted. For here, the 'shirtless and shoeless friends of the

Governor' thronged to applaud him: the ruffians followed him by land- by water too. Those who had hats waved them triumphantly in the air; those who had not, contented themselves with shouts that rent the sky.

As his ship rode down the harbour followed by a crowd of little boats, Bourke stood on deck bareheaded, waving in response to the cheers. Never had a governor of New South Wales been so acclaimed".

Chapter twelve

Thailand

Whenever George saw an Asiatic lad on television he would remark: "He can't be Thai, not good-looking enough". In fact, we shared strongly the belief that Thailand and its people must be the loveliest in the world. How we came to that opinion I cannot explain, since we were far too poor in our early days ever to consider going there, and in his latter years George could not possibly have visited such a hot, humid country in view of his acute asthma. It is the only country in the area never to have been colonised and has a culture that is steeped in Buddhism, mixed with animism and traces of Hinduism.

So on my second visit to Australia in January 1988 I planned to stop over in Thailand and was advised to spend five days in Bangkok and four in Pattaya, 'the premier resort in south-east Asia' as it was then incorrectly called. It was only after I swam in its 'sparkling coral seas' that I read in the "Bangkok Post" that north Pattaya said the sewage system was in south Pattaya and vice versa; actually it was on the drawing board. It remained, alas, a crowded, ugly, seaside brothel, catering for both sexes with unlimited success, but at the terrible price of ruining the lives of many youngsters driven there by dire poverty, especially from North Thailand.

Peter Burton, whom I met in London in 1944 when he was a student at the Royal Academy of Music happened to be visiting Bangkok to see his Thai friend, and was a welcome initial guide to the city's complexities. On my first evening I joined them at Tumnak Thai, then the largest restaurant in the world, it was claimed, with more than 3,000 seats in a pseudo Japanese setting on the outskirts of Bangkok, away from the city's badly polluted districts.

Some of the waiters whizzed by on skates with dishes held aloft, a sight in some ways typifying the Thai delight in merriment, such as I find now at picnics near their second city Chiangmai in the far north at an altitude of 350m. It was founded in 1296 as the capital of Lanna Thai, "Land of a million rice fields".

Peter brought along a pleasant young Thai for me, my first

blind date, and not unacceptable since I was still so very lonely without George. Later we visited "Barbieri", a well known lurid gay bar in the Pat Pong quarter where I was astounded to see about 35 beautiful Thai lads, all in their early twenties – illegal for them to appear under 18 —- wearing only numbered swim slips, little red cuffs and red bow ties. They were waiting, eager to join visitors, especially anyone venturing there unaccompanied. "Where you from?" "What your name?" is their sole approach, later gathering speed, inquiring what your job is, as is allowable in Thailand, even asking how much you earn. "Never enough" you are advised to reply. The final response is "up to you!" when you ask a lad if he is willing to come away for the night. If so, you give the bar about £3 and are told not to give the boy more than about £10 in the morning. Horribly commercial, yet fulfilling a service.

The manager there told me gleefully that he must have Bangkok's best job, selecting the lads on his menu as shown in a photo album and teaching them if necessary. He said all are medically tested regularly, but discarded if not taken out often enough by clients almost exclusively from abroad. "How was number 24?" you may be asked if you return.

During the evening, they present a lurid stage show amusing at times, with drag scenes and macho go-go dancing. After eleven o'clock sex takes place on stage, yet it is illegal to show gay videos, but many places do. At a similar place nearby we later saw young Thais go-go dancing holding metal uprights and doings unmentionable things with their free hands, having wound themselves up, in some cases, while serving drinks at the footlight bar.

Naturally in later years when I occasionally went with Na to such places, he was much embarrassed to see other Thai lads driven to consort with hideous old foreigners. One night he asked me softly could I spare £3 for a young lad he was talking to since he was so very hungry and had no money. It was only at that time, in Bangkok, not in Pattaya or Chiangmai, that lads danced naked. The new Thai Prime Minister had sworn to stop such practices, as did most of his predecessors.

While in Bangkok alone for the first time I naturally went on short tours to see the Royal Palaces, and my favourite "Wat Arun", the temple of the dawn, faced with broken porcelain, standing so majestically over the Chao Phraya "River of the Kings". The sight of a glowing sunset behind it, seen one evening from the other bank is one of my best memories of an otherwise cluttered, discordant city.

There was also an interesting morning tour along evil smelling canals aboard a dangerous long-tailed boat driven by a high-powered car engine attached to a long steering arm. The 'Rose Garden' tour went further afield, pleasantly arranged for short-term visitors who glimpse there Thai dancing, elephant shows and mock marriages set within gardens laden with twin coloured bougainvillaea. I had never expected to see a flower with individual petals red and white on the same stem.

After Bangkok, I went alone to Pattaya. It was January 9th 1988, the day that was to change my life superbly, just as did February 13th 1944 in blacked-out London at Marble Arch.

I checked in at quite a good class hotel and then walked along the sea front. In a quiet spot there stood Na, eating pineapple on a stick, smiling his wonderful smile, while guarding deck chairs. "Hello!", he called out with obvious friendliness, as though he fully expected me to appear. I shall never forget the moment; there stood my new protector, or "second innings" as a Sydney lawyer later dubbed him on seeing a photo. George was presenting his successor. "Here Gerard, will this do?", I could hear him say. "And a Thai boy!" We chatted for a while. He knew a little English since he had worked for a year as a waiter in a restaurant near the infamous "Bridge over the River Kwai", eating scraps left on tourists' plates he later told me, when I asked him why he so seldom cleared completely any of the many little dishes we order when eating together.

It was about four o'clock, so I asked him back to the hotel for a drink from the amply stocked mini bar in my room. "You're not taking him up there!" cried a vigilant lady receptionist, so we decided to have a drink by the pool instead. Then angered by her imperious manner I returned alone and asked on what grounds she was refusing to allow me to take a guest to my room in the afternoon? "It'd be all right if it was a girl", she had the cheek to reply, but then conceded. "How long will you be?" "About an hour, I suppose" I answered. Later, stinging from her haughty attitude, and after my keenest hopes had been beautifully confirmed, I signed him in for the night as he was fortunately carrying sufficient identification.

He told me he was staying for about a month in Pattaya with an aunt whom I met several years later, trying to make some money for his very poor family in the far north. I noticed he would scarcely eat anything while I gorged lobster thermidor, and watched me pay a bill that probably would have kept his whole family for about a week. He then showed me around the town and we watched some Thai kickboxing; he was then 23 and had done the sport in his early days. We arranged to meet three days later but he turned up late. How very fortunate for us both that I waited my maximum 15 minutes – George and I were never late for each other. Then to my delight, he arrived full of apologies, pillion on a motorbike taxi, a common form of transport in Thailand.

For the next two years, I would arrange to meet him in Bangkok on my further visits to Sydney. He would come down by bus from Chiangmai, a ten-hour journey costing under £3 and being about four inches shorter than I, he could curl up cross-legged on the tiny seats and doze en route. It is a dangerous way to go south I hear, being so cheap, as not infrequently the bus is hijacked by bandits, or else tiny Thais crawl up the gangway and rob you while you sleep.

I greatly enjoyed seeing him again, but was very distressed at the brevity of the meetings. Once I asked him not to meet me please before noon, giving myself time to settle in after the long flight. When I arrived at eleven he bounded out from under a bush in the garden where he had been waiting for about two hours. The hotel porters laughed in delight as he threw himself into my arms; in Thailand you can assume that nearly everyone is supportive of the gay way of life. On another occasion, however, when we stayed in a smarter hotel, we were confronted by the guard at the lift every night as we returned from local bars with "You can't bring <u>him</u> in here", wrongly assuming he was a casual pick up. Na would then sternly tell him to please check the residents' list and see whether he was not checked in with Mr. Bourke.

After I had known Na for three years I first went up to visit his home in Maekungnoy village, 16 miles south of Chiangmai. What a wonderful welcome they all gave me! It seemed incredible that his village – simple though it is and the neighbours could all mirror his own attractive qualities. I met his mother Mama Moon, his father Jai and his older married sister Boon and unmarried sister Oot. A perfectly symmetrical family, two gay, two straight, presided over by a serene old grandmother – the Thais revere old age – now dead, alas. Married brother Tong completes the ideal quartet and lives about three miles away.

On their very small farm they grow rice, garlic as a second crop and sometimes a few ground nuts if the weather is suitable; meanwhile they sit weaving baskets or coconut matting, such as we now have on our kitchen floor. As we walked around Na showed me a pile of broken bamboo remnants near the fruit trees and cried pointing out fragments of the frail bamboo house in which he was born and spent his early years. He happened to point out, as we left, a broken swampy hollow near the little river and remarked sadly that he might one day try and build something different there; I said nothing, but the seed was sown.

Before I left after a very simple lunch, Na told me his father had made an appointment for us to go to the village Temple for a blessing on our love from the chief monk, one of his closest friends. His father and brother Tong were both monks for about ten years in their youth, as are most Thai men, even the king was briefly a monk.

It was a wonderful intimate occasion; Na was dressed in a very full white shirt, white or black being their holy colours, and shorts. After greeting Na and I most benignly with a wonderful serenity that spoke more than any words of English could have done, the monk blessed us in turn by tying a saffron sai-sin thread on each of our wrists. Mine watches as I type these words ten years later and guides my hand in proud belief, gratitude and homage.

We stayed four nights in a very good Chiangmai hotel and by day Na took me around pillion on his motorbike, slowly since it was really rather small for two. We went to see them making colourful hand-painted umbrellas at Borsang and to the zoo and the Royal Temple Doi Suteph overlooking the city. However, since it was the "Songkran Festival" in mid-April, we were soaked much of the time. Anyone then is entitled to wish you a happy Thai New Year by throwing a bucket of water over you, or hosing you down. It is about 30°C, so no serious harm is likely to result; only at dusk can one safely dry out.

Pickup trucks with barrels of water replenished from the city's old moat, carry crowds of young Thais fighting passing battles between themselves. "Playing water", Na calls it simply. We also went out to a waterfall, sacred to Thais, where as the only foreigner as far as I could see, I jumped in among them in my clothes. Thais are notorious prudes and rarely like to be seen naked even by their dearest. They never patronise nude beaches, almost non-existent in their otherwise tolerant country.

I was only up there for "Songkran" once more having usually migrated back to Ireland by then. But instead I enjoy Chiangmai's elaborate flower festival each February when there are floral exhibitions in the parks, including very expert bonsai work and a long parade in the morning of floats covered with flowers with great care and precision, depicting often the royal family and doing homage to Buddhism as well. About 40 floats pass round Tha Phae Gate to cheering crowds, including many foreigners there for the occasion.

Early in November, there are similar parades to mark "Loy

Krathong", basically a religious festival with monks giving special sermons, the texts being exhibited on scrolls outside temples. Elaborate hot air balloons are released to whisk away bad luck and to carry one's wishes to heaven. Incoming flights at Chiangmai airport have even been alerted to their presence, so many are released at times.

The wide shallow Ping river is covered with "krathong", floral floats carrying candles and joss sticks and a small coin that will bear away one's wishes for one's family and beloved. Na and I have seen them glide by, released perhaps several miles upstream by whom, for whom? Our prayers follow them on their way.

When the time came to say a sad farewell, I wish I could have known that it would later become my home city too, the happiest place imaginable with three seasons, cool from November to February – farang time – very hot from March to June with heavy rains in the following monsoon months.

So after my sudden unexpected rejection for residency for Sydney, Na was thrilled when I wrote to tell him of my plans to build us a home in his village. He replied sweetly: "Gerard, if you build us a home up here I will always live there most proudly with you!" This promise he has since kept a hundred fold.

I put no restrictions on the plan, but trusted he would be sensible enough not to make it too large or elaborate. I did not then know his superb colour sense, apart from his own very smart appearance, nor the fact that his father, whom I had only met briefly, had studied building while a monk and was an expert craftsman in wood, like so many Thais. Also I did not know what a wonderful team of builders would be available at such very low cost, some were cousins of Na, receiving only about £3 per day for shinning up makeshift bamboo scaffolding, but achieving a far higher standard than I see in Ireland and furthermore only making one house at a time.

Naturally I asked him to buy quickly the little plot from another cousin – Na has about 30 apparently, both parents coming from families of six and the man agreed especially since it was for us lovers, Na told me. The cousin was beaten down in price as is essential for every purchase in Thailand, and expected by the vendor. Planning permission was simple in the extreme; he only had to ask the village headman if it was all right to build there for his foreign friend. (He later told me sadly that if I had changed my mind at this stage he might well have killed himself in disappointment; my poor Na had had such a difficult poor childhood huddled together with his loving family in that often broken bamboo hut, trying to keep out of the rain and gather adequate food.)

So in late October 1991 when I flew up to Chiangmai again and stayed with him a week in the city before going on to Sydney for November and December, he took me out to see the house on which work had started. He had sent me a choice of approximate plans and photos of nearby houses, from which I naturally chose one in true northern Thai style, only with some slight interior European modifications. Little did I suspect that he and his father would themselves design a house so admired locally and by passers by, who sometimes stop to photograph it, to Na's delight.

"Here it is" he exclaimed triumphantly after our motorcycling due south along the big dual carriageway with its superb central dazzle screens of bougainvillaea and eight foot high pointed conifers, neatly trimmed, alternating for several kilometres. He drove carefully, flanked by wild hectic Thai traffic comprising fleets of motorbikes, huge ten-wheel trucks with their drivers often on amphetamines, who flee any accident they cause and innumerable pickup trucks. Relatively few cars are seen, as the purchase price is high. No breathalyser tests are given and only recently have crash helmets been made compulsory. Na unfortunately refuses to wear one yet, though he had a bad accident about six years ago, breaking three ribs and being unconscious for ten hours. "I thought I was dead when I came to in hospital attached to all those tubes", he later told me. Strange to think tigers lurked there until about forty years ago—tiger woods?

We turned down a little potholed road, since well cemented, half way between the market towns of Sanpatong and Lamphun, the ancient capital of the region, with its 1,000 year old Haripunchai temple where brother Tong studied when young. Until recently, it was also chosen as the venue for the annual ladyboy beauty contest with some 200 participants, until stopped by the government. A popular, hilarious evening it was too, by all accounts. We had also passed the ominously named "modern antiques" factory at Hang Dong, a town noted also for its wickerwork.

When I saw the house about a quarter built, I was speechless for once, with delight, without Papageno's padlock on my mouth. Fourteen reinforced concrete pillars rose out of well prepared foundations on a carefully levelled site, overlooked by coconuts, mangoes and lamyai fruit trees, as well as numerous banana plants which are annuals oddly enough, dying down and resurfacing the next year. I watched the carpenters beginning to add the rafters, so I was able to see the superb craftsmanship used throughout, with best hardwood, teak no longer being available, except at enormous expense, thanks to much illegal logging.

Na's father blessed each pillar as it was erected and later placed many sacred signs over the lintels and elsewhere in our splendid home. All his family and many neighbours were gladly lending a hand; Na's mother and sisters were painting, a nice blue, the roof tiles that stood in abeyance leaning against a fence. Later he fetched me a lie-low so I could rest in a corner of our new house on planks laid across some joists, while huge butterflies flew in casually to welcome the new owner from afar. Most importantly too, a little spirit-house had been carefully erected on the river bank as a refuge for those who had been displaced from the site we would so happily occupy in future. It is regularly tended, and furnished with prayer and sustenance for all who abide therein.

Then when I left for two more months in Sydney, sending Na money on different occasions for the work--his father kept strict accounts – I had a dreadful fear that something would go wrong. It seemed utterly impossible that I could ever have the supreme good fortune to live in our own house with my lover. He calls it my house, I call it his; he tried to register it in our joint names but I knew this would not be possible, since foreigners, quite correctly I believe, are not allowed to own property in Thailand.

When I came back in late January, the house was finished and its beauty astounded me, partly due to the 60 blue porcelain uprights round the veranda delivered just before I left, at £2.50 each. The pale-blue wide matching entrance steps are also such an attractive feature. Everything had been bought as cheaply as possible, often directly from factories or from people they knew by repute. Sensible economies were made too, but not in the overall plan, which turned out precisely as I wanted. For example, they originally installed no hot water being totally unused to it themselves in such a very hot climate. Yet in deference to me they had put an English-style toilet, beautifully tiled instead of the treacherous Thai double foot-print type. The shower room was also fully tiled in blue.

They made one Asiatic style sittingroom about 16 ft. square and two bedrooms, one of which we decided to give to sister Oot who does all our laundry and cleaning as well as watering our garden with a herb garden on the river bank and some very sacred bush from which we pick sprigs to place among offerings to the monks. In return she gave us a present of a huge double bed with sides flushed to the floor in the usual Thai style, with a carved headboard with two secure brass-mounted lockers on which she hung a little motif of two yellow bunnies having a bunk-up. Sweet, I thought!

I stood the absence of hot water for about six months but then missing my morning 'think-tank' in Ireland, I decided to install a gas geyser, we cook by gas and resume hot showers, especially since the temperature in November can drop to about 8° at night, though it is back to 28° probably by 10:00 am. It can occasionally freeze on Doi Inthanon, the highest mountain in Thailand due south 30 miles from our village. Na longs to see snow, but I tell him he would not like the related cold.

Our first purchase, appropriately enough on St. Valentine's Day which is keenly observed there, was an ideal set of rattan chairs, a settee and small table, bearing a heart motif, for £80 from a passing truck. We then bought a very good television set which receives five Thai channels on which Na and his sister watch daily two films, or soap operas that are often very beautifully produced.

Each evening we can see for half an hour what the Thai monarchy has been doing that day. King Bhumibol, who has now reigned for fifty years and his family are held in the very highest esteem and take the keenest interest in the well-being of their people. Only in moments of extreme crisis has the King asserted his sovereign powers to great effect. I could see an hour of American news at 8 am but do not bother to do so. Instead, I listen to news bulletins throughout the day on my excellent little short-wave radio.

Being an excellent cook like George, Na goes off daily to little local markets to shop for the family and seek western delicacies for me. For example, he noticed when we were staying in an hotel, I liked croissants, and now searches widely for them; I have not now the heart to say I really do not prize them that much. I never accompany him on these shopping excursions because the stallholders would raise their prices on seeing a foreigner, though he tells them all it is for me he shops so often. They sometimes give him a quick Thai whisky to seal a deal; he apologises on return for being tempted in the afternoon. His motorbike becomes festooned with little plastic bags. Young and old, male and female tell him how beautiful he is apparently and he quickly replies: "Hands off, you know I've Gerard!"

Almost everybody motorcycles between houses, because not

only it is often so very hot, but also because of rabid dogs; not all are taken to the temple to be vaccinated. Once Na was chased up a tree by a rabid dog; I recalled the event recently when reciting psalm 22: verse 20 "Deliver my darling from the power of the dog".

Thais are very proud if genuinely loved by foreigners. In our village of about 300 people, many living in tiny bamboo houses almost hidden in orchards and plantations, there are about four young ladies married to foreigners. In addition, Vichai, a boyhood friend of Na, has a lover Richard, about 55 from Guernsey, but he is often unwell, alas, and is seldom seen, although they live only about 300 yards from us. Yet, when I first went up there he gave me a great welcome saying he usually hated to encounter foreigners but I was an honoured exception.

Na was born on Christmas Eve 1964, just when George and I were preparing two pheasants to eat the next day, our first Christmas back amid the ruin that was then Thornfields. We have a joint birthday party on the festive evening, naturally Christmas is scarcely celebrated in the 95% Buddhist society and Na prepares beautifully a dinner for about 25, mostly gays and family, an occasional ladyboy in drag might appear, too, and is equally welcome. Every village seems to have two or three and they are in no way despised; once when I described gay - bashing to Na, such as might happen in Sydney, he declared even the thought of it would be utterly repugnant to Thais. Drunks fight in discos, as elsewhere, but never about sexual orientation.

Last year Richard and Vichai came to our birthday party; it was pleasant for me, chatting to Richard on the veranda with only Thai spoken around us. Na's family and friends speak virtually no English though a few know a little from their schooldays; others are too shy to try, yet know quite a bit, as does Na's niece, Deun, who presents me her English essays to correct. Na prepares the feast beautifully, careful in its presentation like George used to be, watching that our dishes are not too spicy. Thai whisky, named "Mekong" after the great river, and beer predominates. The whisky is fairly weak but palatable enough when taken with soda and lime. Most lads choose it as the cheapest way to become merry, pliable and amiable – even more so, that is.

The next evening Richard asked us to his home for a Christmas Day party, English style, for the village children and their families charmingly laid out under the fruit trees with fairy lights, paper hats, lucky dips and children's games predominating, with about 150 present. There was no drink except orangeade, suitable for the occasion, balloons flew and fireworks burst around, which Thais love, even those horrid bangers.

We arrived at about 8 o'clock. Na's pals whispered to him "not like your party last night!" and soon he became hungry as little food was in evidence, whereas Thais love to nibble. "Come on Gerard", he whispered. "I'll cook you something at home". His parting shot to Richard was "Many thanks, we're off now. We're Buddhist, you know", a sudden lovely assertion.

On our birthdays we arise early – usually Na gets up about 8 o'clock and I follow at 9 o'clock after he has done some household chores, or earlier if I feel like it. I then warm up on the veranda, which receives direct sunshine only until ten, so perfectly orientated is our home. At 7 o'clock, we go to the Temple to be blessed, usually by a cousin monk. We take small offerings of functional things, even washing powder, all beautifully done up on a tray, in the correct Buddhist manner, including sprigs from a sacred yellow bush growing in our garden. The monk blesses us tenderly together, even asking the time of our births, and gives us each a sai-sin sacred thread for our wrists. An astrological prediction is also included in the simple ceremony.

We take our adopted daughter to be blessed on her birthday, February 12th, in our new five-seater Isuzu pick-up truck. I almost weep with delight to think that I am so honoured to take her there alone with him. Then at lunchtime, we take food prepared in our garden to give lunch and therefore earn merit in the Buddhist belief to about 100 very poor children in the temple school where Na himself once studied. The headmaster thanks us as her parents, and then invites us to lunch with the staff. How very petty and cheap it makes western schools' abject horror of gay relationships.

Sirilac, or Ying to give her her short name as possessed by all

Thais, was born on February 12th 1993 (until about 1913 Thais did not even have surnames, oddly enough). Her mother originally gave her the second name Katae, or little rabbit, but when the baby was unwell soon after birth, she took her to the monks who told her it was because she had given her the wrong second name and that was how she became Ying. On the morning of her birth Na came dashing in to me and threw himself into my arms: "Gerard we have a daughter!" A prime moment in my life.

His brother Tong, two years older, and his wife Kum, already had a daughter Tik, nine years old. But when another baby was coming Na explained that Kum could not cook, to his horror, and did not like babies and since they live in very poor circumstances with a very small rice farm three miles away, the family wondered if we would like to adopt the new arrival, either gender. We were both so delighted at the suggestion, especially since I had noticed when he was in Ireland twice for two months each time in our early days, he always looked for a child to hold when being photographed – a perfect natural father. In preparation, I heard later, he asked a nurse all about vitamins for babies and such, though Ying remained with her natural mother for the first two years and then was gradually introduced to our home which she very quickly preferred. Mama Moon and his sisters nursed her.

Na, or to give him his full name, Chumpon Na Siriwong, correctly obtained official adoption papers for her since, though his brother delighted at the move, he felt she should be the eventual heir to our home, constructed from our love. Na says he also wants her to run messages for him when he is old! She began going to school at two, as is the practice there. No wonder she cried occasionally when setting off, but against that now aged ten she is already very clever especially in arithmetic and art. She raced through 'kiddie snap' long ago without the cards being translated into Thai and before she was three jumped to attention on our veranda and sang the Thai national anthem in perfect pitch. Already she knows the alphabet in Thai and English.

She is so very beautiful, writes "pa-pa Gerard", with big round eyes unlike her sister's that are nearly closed. One neighbour has already asked Na to please keep her for his equally beautiful son: "But she'll be a tomboy" Na replies jokingly. In the early days, it was my job to place her on Tong's motorbike to go home, putting a sacred black mark on her forehead to protect her en route. Often she would cling on, not wishing to return there. It seems terrible to see such tiny children on motorbikes, often squeezed between their parents and perhaps a dog, but they have no other way of getting around.

Nine months after the house was completed Na explained it was time to hold our "Kun ban mai", or house warming and blessing ceremony, a most important part of Thai village culture. Every new house must be blessed to the best of the owner's ability. An uneven number of monks preside, an even number only for funeral wakes.

At first I was shocked to learn it had to be on September 6th, before I returned; but Na explained it had to be on an auspicious day when five special monks would be available, including his father's friend who had blessed us privately two years before. (Na's father can even tell the most auspicious day to plant trees, sow crops or make a deal). The blessing ceremony took place at 7.00 am and really it was best I was not there as I would not have understood the ritual in Thai, in which they prayed for me, too, as the new joint owner. Instead, to my utter delight, Na sent me a beautifully made two-hour video of the great event.

Everyone you have ever met has to be invited to the evening party. Printed cards were distributed to about 250 people. Blue metal chairs were borrowed from the temple, some bearing our joint names to mark a recent donation and blue awnings were erected by the river since it was the rainy season, though fortunately it remained dry.

The previous evening swarmed with activity, preparing food under the trees. All Na's friends turned up to help, as he does frequently for their parties; there was much chopping of buffalo, chickens, ducks and various fiercely spicy dishes. Then at 7:00 p.m. in the evening a short family service was held in our sitting room near our little Buddhist shrine, with monks in attendance, too, and a lay reader saying the ordained prayers.

The main blessing took place the next day from 7:00 am until 8:00 am conducted by five monks, in the presence of all the family and close friends, sitting cross-legged on the floor on very colourful matting, some particular to the occasion. (Looking carefully at the video, I can see Na wiping away tears in a corner, before it all began, overcome by the importance of the occasion, never having dreamt that it would be possible to own his own home there with me. He was looking superb, dressed in a white short-sleeved shirt, fawn slacks and a colourful belt.)

A very long sai-sin sacred thread was then trailed around the house until it encircled the family seated in front on the floor. Na then came forward as the new owner, representing me too, and he wore briefly the white coil of material like a pipe-cleaner on his head, as at a wedding ceremony. Afterwards everyone made merit, giving gifts to the monks, queuing up to do so.

Then at about 6:00 p.m. the guests began to arrive in lively, chatting groups, most smartly dressed. Na was out to greet them all as they appeared by various entrance routes, and a few brought gifts for our new house.

The tables were laid with soft drinks, some Thai whiskey and beer, and there was a simple assortment of biscuits, nuts, fruit and dishes for those who might be hungry, but nothing sweet whatsoever. Thais, especially the young, including our little girl, never eat sweets and so retain their wonderful teeth for many years. Na is proud of his hair; he never has to shave only occasionally to pull out little whiskers from his chin.

A small band had been engaged, doubtless from a cousin and fairy lights shone through the trees; moths sought refuge in our biggest coconut palm. After the meal popular karaoke singing began. Almost no slogan T-shirts were worn, only the smartest matching plain colours, I saw from the video. Naturally, gays and lesbians formed a good proportion of the guests, there were about five guys in drag there too, he told me. Na sang three times – he loves doing so – and welcomed and thanked the guests from me, too, I am sure. Apparently, his father had wisely told him not to drink a drop himself that evening in case it might suddenly affect him in his great excitement. "Oh, my father, Poh Jai, knows all about this world and the next", he solemnly declared one day, in a loving tribute to his Dad, who sometimes prepares elaborate Buddhist charts to keep in my pocket to protect me on journeys and similar ones adorn the house.

When I look at the video I think it wonderful that almost every villager attended to bless the house I made out of my enduring love for Na. He often tells me how much they love me and wish they could talk to me in English. Just as when I first went up there he made certain I met everybody at once, including an old cousin selling water melons by the road, as we drove out the first morning. Never once have I received an adverse look on being introduced, even to a beautiful young dentist, as his Irish lover. Such is the Thai acceptance of sexual orientation.

When in Chiangmai we always stayed at "Top North" guesthouse with about 100 rooms and a small swimming pool, going in for a few days every three weeks to give Na a break from cooking and shopping. We soon realised neither of us wished to visit the city's gay bars and gave them a wide berth. The owners gave us a pleasant air-conditioned room for £10 nightly. There was a restaurant, but no television, so when wishing to see the Australian Open Tennis in January I would have to drink in a nearby girlie go-go bar that had a satellite TV corner.

At least there I was able to say "Sorry, I'm gay" if any girl ventured to approach me hopefully, at a critical match point. "That's alright, dear", she'd reply, moving on to a more likely conquest. (Na once saw in his Thai paper, not given in the "Bangkok Post", a picture of an American vicar, 73, dead in room number 109 in "Top North". "Silent Murder", it was headed. Apparently, he had been seen taking back a different lad every night not on church funds, I hope, until he chose a dud who smothered and robbed him. "Gerard, please don't ever book that room", Na pleaded. "There would be a ghost inside it".)

Then I had the luck to talk to a German, my age, who told me that the 450 room "Diamond Hotel" overlooking the Ping river had a new eat-all-you-can buffet for £5 and invited me to join him there. Frankly I was amazed. Surrounded by orchids in flower, the restaurant presented every oriental and western delicacy you could wish to find, flambé here, barbecued seafood there, including crabs and enormous king prawns. Tables were laid with smart linen cloths and attentive beautiful waiters were at hand to deflect mayfly hatching out on the river bank from landing on your shoulder, or in your soup. There is a huge old tree overhanging, since partly obscured by fairy lights, and a large spirit-house beside it, in homage to the spirits displaced when the hotel was built.

Later after several visits there, my favourite waiter was sent over as soon as I was sighted dining alone. He asked my name, and then showed me his tag with about 15 letters, "but they call me Kit", he said shyly and my dear friend Kit Rohan had died just shortly before. Now I am becoming accustomed to such strange coincidences, if such they be. (When he went off to fetch my order, I called after him "my pet!", since it only meant "not too spicy, please" in Thai).

Some months later as I sat there a smartly dressed Thai sat down beside me and asked in good English, where I came from and was I there long as he had seen me often. After I told him how much I loved Thailand, and had built a house for my Thai friend – emphasising the word – and our adopted baby, south of Chiangmai, he turned round the conversation. "Where do you stay when you come into Chiangmai some weekends?" "In "Top North" I replied, "for £10 a night". "But you don't have TV there for watching tennis do you? After what you've told me you've done for that very poor family, you can have a room here, at a special rate with satellite TV in your room". Whereupon he showed me one of the best hotel rooms I have ever stayed in, with three-speed silent air conditioning, a power shower, bath and immaculate linen changed daily. I have the full hotel facilities including a 25m swimming pool. usually deserted since Thais never sun-bathe or swim during the day not wanting to become brown like the Burmese, as Na explains. Melanoma is very rare in Thailand.

I always have my motorbike, the excellent 110cc Honda

"Dream" three gear automatic, electric starter, when staying there and often drive out to Krista Doi pleasure gardens as the Victorians would have called them, partly sponsored by the monarchy. There Thais and a very few foreigners gather to admire the fine floral displays. There is no public transport there and apart from the Thai New Year, it is never crowded. A new rose garden is now added, lined with elegant pointed conifers; children used to ride elephants along the wider paths, but do so no longer. It saddens Na much to see these noble beasts so degraded, especially sometimes driven along city streets with slogans painted in white on their sides.

The very helpful Royal Thai Consulate in Dublin give me a maximum six month visa, possibly because I did the correct thing and introduced Na there when he came here firstly. They also know about my Thai house and our little daughter, which pleases them. I just have to show I am financially independent as a condition of the extra three months on a non-immigrant visa. However, I do have to leave Thailand, even for five minutes, before the first three months expires.

The first year we turned the occasion into a lovely holiday on Koh Samui island, by far the most beautiful Thai resort I have seen. It is off the south-east coast and is the chief source of coconuts for Bangkok. But more importantly its beauty is maintained by the strict rule that no building may be higher than their fine palms. It was there that Na first warned me not to rest immediately below one.

We flew to the most southerly airport in Thailand, Hat Yai, and then took a taxi to the Malaysian border through dense rubber plantations. There I crossed in and out of Malaysia having my visa stamped, before we took the train north to Surat Thani, my first long train journey there, five hours on hard seats, Na having booked third class by mistake.

After a memorable night in the port for Koh Samui in a palatial new hotel, which Na beat down to £20 for the night, we took the large ferry out to Koh Samui. The sea was calm – on a rough passage on Bangkok's dirty canals, poor Na had once been a trifle sea-sick partly out of anxiety – and it was my first sighting of those startling limestone outcrops that stand erect in the sea, tropical pinnacles of great charm and wonder, like Chinese mountains of the deep.

We had been advised to stay in the northern sheltered Bay of Bohput at the grandly named "World Resort", where we had a very comfortable chalet directly by the sea for £10 a night. There was a good swimming pool also, little used, with several bars, satellite TV and little Thai restaurants where Na could chat away.

Although I had read in "The Bangkok Post" that anyone foolish enough to hire a motorbike on the island's one circular route, is likely to be sent back in a bodybag, we did so, but only for a day, since the road is barely wide enough for two cars and has a drop of about a foot at the edge, horrendous for a motorcycle pushed aside by racing cars. There were frequent signs to local hospitals en route.

There was only one suitable day tour, to a superb marine park lying not far off shore, lunch provided on board. We were taken ashore to various small islands by longtail boat. The sea was quite rough and I missed the leap aboard, flying into the sea headfirst much to the general amusement. As always Na drew much attention partly because, little knowing, he chose to wear shorts printed in an "American Express" design. "Look what he's bought with his card"; I could imagine being whispered nearby. Anyhow, as we came ashore from the trip, I noticed a man holding on high a plate with Na's face smiling down; everybody had been photographed going onboard in the hopes of a sale afterwards. At least they found one eager customer.

We also went south for two days to Lamai resort, noisy, windy, and with a strip of raunchy jazz halls and bars, about two miles from where we stayed. It was a Saturday afternoon when Na told me that two young waiters had invited him out for the evening to show him the haunts. I was horribly torn between letting him off to enjoy himself, and wondering would he be all right. He could naturally see how worried I was. Anyhow, to my delight he returned about 15 minutes later to say the lads were going four on one motorbike and he did not think it safe. How very relieved I was.

Finally, we flew back to Bangkok and thence up to Chiangmai by the small "Bangkok Airways" in a 50-seater plane that left a tiny airport only 15 minutes drive from our hotel. Na had much news and excitement to tell his family on our return, which is his highlight of any holiday we undertake. Another wonderful trait in his character.

The next January we broke my six months by holidaying by air to Penang, an expensive trip but well worth it in every way; an Australian friend had strongly advised me to stay on the island's only northern beach at the "Golden Sands", but the brochure he sent, already four years old, listed rooms at about £100 a night. It had been opened 10 years earlier by the Prime Minister and commands a splendid view with spectacularly grouped swimming pools amid thatched hut refreshment stalls.

Not wanting such extravagance, thinking of our village costs, we decided to fly down and book a room on arrival at the airport. We chanced on the "Lone Pine Hotel" and luckily booked it only for two nights. Just as well, since it turned out very unsatisfactory, with a bed with springs badly broken – not by us – no pictures whatsoever and cold water. The beach itself was all right until we saw them trying to revive there a Japanese lady who was killed when she fell off one of those large inflated banana-shaped boats. But it was exactly beside the "Golden Sands""

After our reserved nights, I went into its reception hall, very grandly designed and chanced I think on a gay lady receptionist. I told her how inadequate the neighbouring hotel had been and asked how much in fact would a room be there, not wishing to spoil our holiday. "Oh, if you don't mind one facing the hills, not the sea", she replied smiling, "I have a very nice double which I would discount to £75 or £50 since your friend is Thai". Naturally, I accepted at once the beautiful room she insisted on showing us in advance.

How happily we lived it up for the ensuing week; Na looked superb as always in the grandeur that he never found awesome in the least. One evening he was enthralled watching a fashion show in the lounge and by day we swam, late for Na and watched paragliding and horse riding on the beach. The former no, but I should have put him up on the piebald horse he had held so proudly. To our disappointment we found no Thai spoken – Thailand is not so far away – or available Thai food.

After much research, I found an alternative easy and cheap way to go out of Thailand before my three months were up. I sent my passport down to Bangkok by agent's courier to obtain a visa for Laos, costing about £40. It is too risky to have it waiting at the border as an American told me who had had his passport held to ransom by officials who crudely demanded an extra £100 to give it back.

Then I caught the 6:00 am bus from Chiangmai to Chiangkong, £5 return, the border town on the Thai bank of the great Mekong River that divides the two countries. The 70-seater single deck bus, with fan ventilation, takes six hours to get there, and stops every 90 minutes for relief of any kind. You need to be small since it is rather cramped, but the Thais greatly enjoy seeing an old foreigner in their midst and are wonderful communicators with their varied smiles. The journey is quite mountainous at first, so I did not encourage Na to come with me, since he tends to have travel sickness.

On arrival at Chiangkong I had two hours before the bus returned in which to take a motorbike taxi down about half a mile to the river passport control where I was stamped out of Thailand, before taking a solo trip in a longtail boat, by sign language, across the mighty swirling river. Then I hurried up a steep flight of slippery steps to the Laotian control office, had my passport stamped in and out of Laos, and filled in a form saying generously that I had stayed there half a day, in their delightful country. "See you longer next year" I lied. I took the same ferryman back across the Styx. To the same Thai border control man I revealed myself again within about 10 minutes and took a motorbike back to the departing bus. I just had time to eat fried rice, duck and a drink of orange for 50p, as had been the motorbike, the ferry and anything else there it seemed.

It all depended on none of the participants having a midday siesta; should I have missed the only return bus, there would have been but one inferior hotel to find. Back at 9:00 p.m. in Chiangmai,

194

the hotel staff were amazed to hear that I had been to Laos for the day, at the age of 74. Not a page of my books had I read I so love to watch Thais at work or play; their gentle calm posture when walking, or in contemplation, is a joy to behold. This system for renewing my visa worked fine for two years, but was a disaster the third time. Na saw me off on the very early bus and I told him I would be back at 8:30 p.m. Half way there, the bus broke down among the mountains and the driver had to excavate the centre panel to start the diesel flowing again. Perhaps it had become too cold. That delayed us twenty minutes and I dreaded every-subsequent laboured gear change. On the return trip worse befell us, the bus emptied its load of diesel onto the road and we were abandoned at a filling station for about two hours until a replacement bus appeared. (I am as allergic to diesel fumes as to passive smoking and soon I had no voice left at all). A young girl took me pillion, in sign language, so I could try to leave a message at our hotel to inform Na I would be back, but very late. He was never given it. When I ultimately arrived at eleven he was there terrified, not able to watch television in comfort lest he missed a call. Next time we will fly together to Laos instead.

I have at last fully discarded my early scientific training and learned not to seek a reason for everything. I accept Anatole France's dictum "Chance is the pseudonym God uses when he does not want to sign his name". So it  was at Dingle shortly after George's death when Dan said to me "Gerard, look inside that nice new Catholic Church" and I soon reeled out to tell him I had seen enough. The last Station of the Cross had the figure of St. George and underneath I read "Do not weep for me". Now it has happened again in an amazing way, some may be sceptical, I am not.

Na chose me a lovely Thai gold pendant to be worn by the

head of our little family – as usual it could be returned less 15% at any time if needs be. (Some richer Thais even invest in Thai gold watching its fluctuation). Inside the locket, he placed without asking, a miniature of Luang Bu Waen, a greatly revered abbot monk who lived not long ago near Chiang Dao, some 30 miles north of Chiangmai. He was known to have acquired through meditation and devotions far beyond the normal, rare psychic powers including the ability to transport himself from place to place at will, a form of levitation.

This strange ability became widely known when two Thai airforce officers were flying over the area and to their astonishment they saw him sitting on a cloud in an attitude of serene contemplation. So astounded were they that they sought out within the area below this arahat, or man of supreme wisdom and truth. Accounts and verification of the monk's amazing powers spread quickly throughout the north, even the King went to pay homage to Luang Bu Waen.

Later a wealthy Thai, wishing to earn further merit, decided when Luang Bu Waen died to ask Madame Tussaud's wax-works to make a replica, measurements having been made during his last illness. This they did and hearing the strange account of his wonderful life, made it for half-price on condition they could keep a copy.

Then I happened to see in the "Bangkok Post" about the extensive caves near Chiang Dao, not far from the monk's temple, inside which are Buddhist shrines executed many centuries ago. I showed Na the beautiful photos and article, and we decided to go there on a family picnic the following Sunday. I wore my Thai gold pendant surprisingly on a day of cave exploration, as I usually reserve it for safer parties at which elderly Thais are delighted to see their Luang

Bu Waen within the locket. Our little daughter came with us and greatly enjoyed the excursion into the vast caverns with the shrines skilfully placed to be illuminated by shafts of sunlight from holes above. Later Na took most of the family off to eat hot food, spicy that is, at little stalls scattered around. There were few people near me as I sat in the sunshine. Only brother Tong sat on a bench opposite my position.

Then to my utter astonishment, for I had seen no one approach, Luang Bu Waen – for surely it was he, though somewhat younger than in the photo – stood before me, and immediately smiled down at my locket and remarked "Nice to see you wearing that" and was gone. He had vanished. I would have seen him walk away. I was absolutely stunned, since it was a clear vision bestowed upon me. Was it for this then that I had worn the pendant that day? If so, what a tribute to my deep love for the Thai people and their devout beliefs. It transpired that Tong had seen nothing at all, though sitting only a few feet in front of me. I still recall the episode with awe. I give no explanation. I find none necessary, or possible.

Now for a few impressions of life at Maekungnoy, the loveliest of villages where Na was so lucky to be born, as he always asserts. He and his sister Oot both dress so nicely having 40 or more T-shirts they share; no item of clothing is ever worn twice without being washed by her – she pushes the little washing machine into the yard to work. When he appears looking so beautiful I sometimes say "Oh, Na, you look so beautiful today". Invariably he replies disarmingly "I hope so". Quite often he goes off to parties in other villages at night, leaving at about 8:00 p.m. but only after he has made sure that I have had my supper. (I admit I have never been allowed to wash up a cup – utterly spoiled). There is always a large plate of rice before me and then a choice of about six other dishes, not too spicy for my farang taste. He had also cooked at 6:30, on returning from the little markets for his family who sit cross-legged on the floor around small circular kantoke tables.

Their very hot food often includes hot buffalo and other specialised dishes and they have 'sticky rice' which they prefer, sometimes cooked in hollow bamboo canes. Often we begin with about

25 huge king prawns, very cheaply bought since they are farmed successfully there, as with much other seafood. Fresh, too, since usually bought alive. The actual large kitchen building about ten-feet from the main house, we added after the first two years so that cooking merriment and fumes do not come into the main house. It also has a Thai toilet and shower room at the back for family use.

Na always tell me what party he is going to exactly, or if it is a funeral how the gays will gather to make the paper funeral flowers, a job left exclusively to them it seems. He apologises for not taking me, but explains no-one would speak any English. Being afraid of bandits on the road and ghosts to a degree, he likes to go with other motorcyclists when possible. Once a friend of his was held up by a bandit who wanted to take his motorbike; they carry no tax plates for six months and meanwhile are hard to trace. He took a stone and killed the bandit, and was going to get about twelve years in prison, though later I heard the sentence had been much reduced.

Sometimes I like to take a census sitting on the veranda at about half past five, before sister Oot arrives with a beer and nuts, spring rolls or fresh pineapple. It is always 30 motorbikes, eight pickup trucks, one cyclist and no motor car or pedestrian in a half hour. After dark no one passes by since everyone reaches their destination early. It is then, too, that Mama Moon often  arrives with little Sirilac all spruced up, being presented to play with me, as though by a Victorian nanny. Oh what a joy to welcome my little 'Siamese kitten' – Thailand was called Siam until 1939. So I then play happily with the god-child of dear 'Mama Nancy', as Na once christened her.

Sister Oot washes my motorbike about every third day, though I tell her Irish ones are never so honoured. Na washes and polishes the car every time it is used, before putting it under a dust sheet in the car-port. Now he has built a new little bridge, in matching blue, over the river so we can drive in more easily, its very old predecessor was so groggy, guests were sometimes afraid to chance it.

Sometimes Na's father comes up with candles, and lights them in front of our shrine where I pray with him. He intones Buddhist prayers and I join in the actions, praying most thankfully for his giving me his son as lover. Initially I asked Na to make sure his family knew all about George, and that he was my chosen replacement.

Occasionally someone will come to see Na and wish to stay the night, to go home safely at dawn. Na's mother then prepares him a mattress and blanket on the floor of our sitting room. Most nights I retire at about 9.30 while Na and his sister and perhaps Sirilac, watch Thai soap operas and Chinese films crowded with ghosts. Na joins me around 10.15 leaving his sister to see more movies; if too loud, he shouts at her through the thin dividing wooden wall. Being illiterate, poor dear, the television has an added importance for her.

Na long tried to obtain a telephone, but it has only recently come to our delight, since it is of vital importance in our partial isolation. Vichai has a portable phone so Richard can phone him from Guernsey; but unlike Na he does not stay with his family while Richard is away, but goes into Chiangmai or down to Pattaya.

The average income of parents with two children is about £8 a week I have read, and nobody sees £1,000 usually in their lifetime and there is absolutely no social security. Only now are they thinking of giving a £5 a month old age pension. Sometimes Na hurries to give a meal to a passer-by who badly needs it. On the other hand, his family would help someone in farming difficulties - communal support is vital.

George taught me not to ask questions if you do not want to hear the answer. For the first year or two I refrained from asking the actual size of their tiny farm, or whom he slept with in my absence. Then, perfectly in character, he looked at me solemnly, reading my thoughts just as George always did and remarked before I left "You know Gerard while you are away I will only be sleeping with my mother or father". I suppose he knew I would wonder who would meanwhile be favoured to see the first rays of light adorn that lovely face each morning.

Among the many simple delights while staying at our house - how it has the complex number 110/M/9 I will never understand since no other houses seem numbered at all - are watching armadas of lively ducks, including many beautiful big Muscovies, enjoying our little river - on which kingfishers flash by while Mama Moon's broody hen with a full complement of chickens chases ants among the leaves. Kites are merrily flown especially in the gentle march winds; one almost became entangled round my neck on its string one day, causing ample giggles from its young owner. Lads carry cock(erel)s under their arms on motorbikes, off to one of many cock fighting areas I carefully avoid. Some are trained in a neighbours' garden for this horrid sport on which much betting takes place.

Our little terrier Bic rolls playfully but never barks unlike our first dog who did so frequently precisely under our bed where he chose to sleep in the four-foot space required for coolness under a correctly constructed northern Thai house. We also have galae emblems of entwined buffalo horns, seen locally on many roof-top peaks. Boc, the companion of Bic and very alike, went missing, eaten we feared by some Chinese living not far away. 'Dog Food' has a different connotation when we see it over shops at times. At first, I used to see people fishing in our small river with nets, electric poles attached to car batteries, and even shooting the tiny fish in desperation. Recently they rest in peace, or do not now exist there.

Snakes are few fortunately. One day Na just managed to miss both ends of a very large one lying in our tracks; as a Buddhist he would never kill wantonly. I have not yet eaten snake, as far as I know, but fox I have enjoyed more than once, also part of a special locust omelette Na was making for his mother, a bad diabetic. Formerly she used to have to be taken for her monthly check-up at the hospital six miles away at Sanpatong pillion on his motorbike, but now I am delighted to say she is taken in our new Isuzu pickup, 90hp, which Na has not yet ventured to drive in fifth gear. It did 5,000 miles in the first two years. He likes to drive in bare feet.

Two years ago at Christmas she was very ill with typhoid, it was eventually diagnosed. At first the doctor would come, by motorbike, three times a day to change her drip-feeds. Monks and a herbalist would also try village cures. Ultimately her sons took her in to Chiangmai to a very good American-run hospital where she was cured after about three weeks. There members of her family had to maintain a rota to assist the nursing, as is common in the orient, sometimes sleeping under her bed and eating on the floor.

Medical services in general I have found excellent. When I broke a front tooth on holiday in Koh Samui after neighbours came to gape and giggle at its absence, Na took me to a local dentist who replaced it and the next one that was groggy for £25, after an anxious start when I saw him preparing to use an ancient pedal-drill, working at home in front of his admiring old mother, to avoid paying tax. He was well qualified from Chiangmai's excellent university, founded in 1963.

Another time an Australian friend observed my left eye was almost totally bloodshot and remarked ominously what if it had been a vein in my brain that had burst - just as I was beginning a nice roast duck dinner. He took me at once to a leading eye specialist whose full examination in hospital and treatment only cost three pounds. Later another charming Chiangmai doctor gave me a chest examination, two X-rays upstairs and medication from his own pharmacy all for eight pounds. I have now learned not to take out costly medical insurance for Thailand, where furthermore, all doctors must speak English by law. The most terrible aspect of medicine in Thailand now is the awful spread of Aids. Seven years ago some Thais still denied its existence; the programme of education has really come too late to save many lives, young and old. Our north west region is alas about the worst affected too. I read that Sanpatong hospital had 300 cases three years ago and now about 1,500. Na goes to Aids related funerals very often, and the plague is continuing with many cases arriving from Burma or China to exacerbate the problem. It is mostly heterosexual now and often caused by husbands wandering off to brothels.

Among the most surprising delights seen from my veranda where I take the salute from so many waving friends, was when one afternoon three teenage lads dressed in wonderful Thai silks passed by trotting on little ponies similarly clad. I was so amazed I did not think to grab my camera, usually at hand. Na told me later they would have been circling their home village for the last time before going off to become monks, perhaps short term or forever. If they had been younger they would have been led by, or younger still, gone to the temple piggy back on their fathers' shoulders. What joyous tales I hear.

Another stunning sight was when about 30 middle aged or older ladies danced trance like again beautifully clad, to a small gamelan rhythmic band almost all day nearly opposite our home. Na told me they were dancing thus to drive away an evil spirit seriously affecting one of their friends.

How I wish I could speak their language. I went so far as buying a Thai linguaphone set but found it of little use, my hearing not now being sufficiently good for the minute inflections that can totally change the meaning of a word, also my memory is lacking as the years speed by. I have, however, amassed sufficient courtesy Thai and can by now ask for various foods when I stop while out motorcycling, at little mountain cafés where probably no foreigner ever paused before.

The loveliest drive I take alone when staying in Chiangmai is up Doi Suteph mountain directly overlooking the city to "Wat Phra That" royal temple. It is about five miles up the mountain and noticeably cooler with superb views of the valley below. Most foreigners go up in "two rowers", as the open mini buses are called with passengers facing each other in frail metal vehicles. I have found these far too dangerous, driven fast downhill - Na was terrified in one once, clinging to me as though in free fall.

There are about eight very sharp hairpin bends on the road constructed only in 1936, giving general access to the wonderful temple for the first time. (Different sections were made, to earn merit, by different nearby communities). The site was originally chosen by King Ku Na in the 14th century for a temple repository for holy relics then unearthed. To find the correct auspicious spot the relics were placed on the back of an elephant. (A royal white elephant, property of the king, is still occasionally encountered, as at the elephant hospital we visited near Lampang. It is so called only because its toe nails are white and other slight variations). When it was released the powerful elephant, very numerous in those days, but not now, lumbered off almost to the top of the mountain where it trumpeted, turned round three times and knelt down as if in prayer. So was the venerable site chosen, it is still believed.

When I drive up alone I watch the tall dry grasses by the side knowing that at least in theory, a tiger might be peeping out to oversee my pilgrimage on high. This would be more likely however if potions made from desiccated tigers penises were not on sale in a hill-tribe village, rather artificially assembled, on the mountain top above the King's summer residence, Phuping Palace, where one can see the royal gardens in his absence.

Nevertheless, I go up to pray, meditate and give thanks, in this incredibly tranquil setting. I now know sufficient about Buddhist ceremonials to take part correctly in simple rituals. I buy my lotus flower - recycled of course - joss sticks and tiny pieces of gold leaf to apply correctly for about a pound. Then I pray among worshipping Thais and an occasional foreigner; sometimes I am blessed by an aged monk in a side chapel who sprinkles me with holy water and ties a sacred sai-sin thread on my left wrist. Once Na's father was very pleased to see an extra one on my return from this famous place.

I also walk three times round the huge central golden chedi in which the sacred relics are entombed and later admire the intricate old murals. Coming down is the problem but I descend very carefully in second gear and well to the side to avoid frantic rattling taxis and huge coaches.

Only once have I been to a Thai wedding. The sister of Anun, a former head waiter at the Diamond Hotel, but now doing hairdressing at home for about 50p a time, was marrying. About 200 were present at the party out under fruit trees, as usual, where I was again the only foreigner. The actual civil ceremony takes place in private early in the morning within the home. On our arrival, Anun placed us at four or five little tables where we were soon joined by other gays en masse - both the bride's brothers being so, rather to their mother's sorrow, I learned. Na, I think, would have known the true gender of almost everyone present. On our return from the happy occasion he told me delightedly: "Gerard, I told all the old ladies it was our eighth anniversary and you no butterfly, and they all gave us the thumbs up and wished us well". Typical Thai respect for love.

One evening I was eating alone out of doors in a pleasant quiet little Italian restaurant, most are German or English orientated, when a most upsetting occurrence took place. A little boy about seven years old crept up beside me and snatched a bread roll from my side plate. It reduced me to tears, as when on my return from the city one day, our little Sirilac ran to me and prostrated herself before me in love and gratitude.

The afternoon before I leave, at five o'clock precisely, senior members of our family specially dressed for the occasion, come to bless me by our shrine. A shirt of mine is placed on a platter, on which are then placed two sacrificed chickens. I hold out each wrist in turn, placing the other palm beneath my elbow for sacred threads to remain there for at least a week.

While the house was being built I rightly thought I should read again "Out of Africa" by Karen Blixen, whom I once met in Copenhagen, very frail by then, dressed entirely in black. For at times, as I anticipated, I feel exactly her contentment in a similar village situation. Strange, too, that one evening at dusk reading Charlotte Brönte's "Jane Eyre" I should meet this passage: "To live amidst general regard, though it be but the regard of working people, is like sitting in sunshine, calm and sweet serene inward feelings bud and bloom under the rays".

I am unfortunately not wise in literature, but there are a few favourite passages nevertheless. Alan Bennett, a convert to

Buddhism, writes, "The most important virtue, by far, is divine compassion". Evelyn Waugh in "Brideshead Revisited" commented: "To know and love one other human being is the root of all wisdom". Finally, when cynics ask me how I can love my Na at such a distance when in Ireland, I am ready with Goethe's "Friends are not only together mentally when they are together physically".

But my most enjoyable veranda reading by far has been Proust's "Remembrances of Things Past". Where else would I have had the time and opportunity to savour every one of those long sentences so beautifully constructed, even to reading quietly to myself some I especially liked, and at, I believe the right age to do so? I was delighted that two good friends had separately advised me to read this great undertaking.

Shortly before I returned in October 1996, Na wrote to me that a neighbour was soon selling his little fruit farm of longans with ten mature trees and room for about thirty more. He wondered whether I might be interested in trying to buy the place as it was beside where Sirilac was born, and the owner had known them all his life. He, too, had been born very poor but had by now improved his position by hard work.

The luscious fruit grown there, sweet white-fleshed husk covered rather like lychees, are much prized especially since they only grow within about 100 miles of Chiangmai and especially well in Na's area. He and his brother try to deal in them, buying up small orchards if they have enough capital but have never owned any themselves. So fortunately I was careful to take with me a savings certificate of appropriate size in case the idea proved worthwhile.

On arrival, I discussed it fully with Na, and it seemed a wonderful opportunity to provide some security for him when I am gone, in addition to legacies. He did not take me to see the place since he knew that if a foreigner appeared the owner might increase the price. Instead Na and his father had several meetings with him and eventually persuaded him to reduce the price considerably, explaining how they would look after it well, and use every square yard. It is very well watered, yet can never flood and is right by a road with easy access. Brother Tong can see it from his home, and their father said he would make a little hut on it if we bought it, so he could make sure no one stole any fruit when ripe, by sleeping there. A mature longan tree can bear as much as £70 worth of fruit in a good year. Na asked him "Would you not be afraid of the ghosts at night"? (But Na has not yet been a monk himself and says he will probably be so when he has someone to pray for - a very consoling thought).

After several weeks, he told me sadly that a Thai doctor was now asking to buy the orchard as an investment, as well as a third man. Our hopes were dashed, since surely they would easily outbid us. The asking price had been £15,000 but that was bargained down to £12,000 over many Thai whiskies. It already brings an annual income of £500 and after ten years should be yielding about £2,000 annually, a huge sum by their standards.

I explained to Na, for the first time, that it was a large sum for me to find, after the house and car, being neither rich nor poor. He fully understood I could never again fund such a sum for any purpose. Yet it was too good an opportunity to miss. Now, to my absolute delight, we own it, the vendor having refused the doctor's higher bid being a man of high Buddhist principles, and a long-time friend.

At last, I visited the lovely spot, carefully surveyed anew by the authorities with new deeds drawn up in Na's name and our daughter as heir. Seeing Na dance with delight among his own longan trees that he never thought to own, I told him truthfully I was as happy as though it had been given to me. We had not gone away the whole five months but stayed around trying to make certain to achieve this goal.

Another occasion comes to mind. One day parents came to our home on their motorbike with a little boy, about three, wedged between them. They wanted to consult Na's father, as the boy had been unwell. They knew, as a former senior monk, he would be able to perform a healing cure. I watched from a distance as he took a glass of water - we have excellent spring water at our home luckily - blew on it, and gave it to the young lad to drink. One more similar visit only was needed. Na later told me he had often been similarly cured when young. What lovely active faith!

On December 10th, my 75th birthday, we went at 7.00a.m. as is customary, to be blessed with our little daughter by the head monk, or abbot, only about 25 years old and a close friend of ours, who frequently comes to chat with Na's father, sometimes bringing young acolytes with him - charming serene groupings.

Then at noon we again gave lunch, to earn merit, to about 95 very poor children at the temple school. They had been told not to bring lunch that day. Other gays and relations of Na helped us prepare the food out under the trees on braziers, before we took it down in our pickup truck. The little children quickly gathered into lines among the bougainvillaea, in front of old lorry tyres representing the Buddhist wheel of life. The headmaster thanked us both and the little children, so beautifully dressed and smiling, sang "Happy Birthday" in Thai and English. Na tells me we are the only people to continue this ancient tradition in our village. I am very well rewarded when these same children on other evenings call out and wave, seeing me reading alone as dusk falls quickly 20° north of the equator.

Sirilac was accepted for her new Sanpatong School during this visit. It is co-educational with about 600 pupils. Na took her with her natural mother, explaining we had adopted her and applied for entrance. There were 100 applicants for only 30 places he later told me. So lots were drawn. The clever little girl walked up and drew "Yes". The fees are £125 for a year's tuition at the day school, including a meal a day, two red school uniforms and her books - it can be paid in two halves if necessary. She had to have her ponytail cut off by her father for attendance, alas, it was so beautiful; but she was so keen to attend she did not mind the loss at all. At her previous school, shortly before she left, the teachers implored us to let them enter her for a "Miss Kindergarten Sanpatong" beauty contest despite her age. Na came back to tell me delightedly that she was fourth out of 53.

At our supper party for my birthday, the abbot brought me a statue of the Buddha, encased and inscribed for my 75th birthday to place upon our sitting room shrine, a lovely acceptance into their religion. That very day, too, I had the enormous pleasure of seeing Sirilac take two little pieces of chalk and draw different pictures with each hand on a make-do slate. How amazing that she is evidently ambidextrous like me; am I to believe it is to show she was born for Pa-Pa's care?

An enjoyable addition in Chiangmai that time was an excellent new gay restaurant "The Gate" run by Natee, a delightful young Chinese-Thai from a wealthy family and a former gay activist in Bangkok. He acted the perfect patron, too, introducing one to other foreigners, or young Thais, as seemed more appropriate. It was my dear friend John Haylock, a member of a small quorum of European friends I now have there, who kindly told me about the place. "A favourite Thai take-away", I dubbed it.

John has wintered partly in Chiangmai in an apartment of the Rincome Hotel for about ten years and is charming company for us both. I have also had the pleasure of entertaining him at Thornfields twice, a most engaging, witty, companion who has often invited me to meet Europeans staying with him in his apartment. The first time he came out to see our house he brought me a copy of his novel "A Touch of the Orient" set partly in the city and on sale there also is his equally engaging one about foreigners' exploits in Laos, "It's all your fault".

Anyone 'touched by the orient' has fallen in love with it and its people, as earnestly as we have. On the flyleaf he had written: "For Gerard, who was touched, ventured and found joy. In admiration. John". And so it was.

Finally, I reflect that when my great-aunt Lucy, youngest daughter of the governor died in 1823 aged only 13, the local rector of Abington, Charles Forster, wrote a beautiful 34-verse eulogy for her and her afflicted family. It included the verses:

"Yes, Thornfields, dear domestic seat,
Sweet refuge from life's angry smart,
While tempests rolled and billows beat,
To thee, we turned "to rest the heart"!
See, round the hospitable board
Congenial minds in converse blend

Such converse as befits thy lord,
  Of Burke the kinsman, pupil, friend.
Also of little Lucy he wrote especially:
  "Whose heart was formed to love but few
  To love but few and love these well".

I hope that this may also be said of me.

Chapter thirteen

Visits to Laos. Au Revoir.

In view of the horrible third bus journey I made alone to Laos from Chiangmai to renew my visa in January 1997, when the vehicle broke down frequently, Na and I decided to fly there instead to celebrate our tenth anniversary the following year. The country is the size of Britain but has a population of only five million people, divided into some fifty ethnic groups; it was once known as "The land of a million elephants", and 70% of the terrain is mountainous with many high plateaux. The Mekong river flows for almost 2,000 km through the land, forming the border with Thailand on its west, much of the way.

Now controlled by a one-party People's Democratic Republic founded in 1975, it has been among the poorest countries in the world with only about 15,000 visitors annually, but over the last decade it has endeavoured to attract more people, though maintaining high visa charges. There is a new 'Friendship Bridge' near the capital Vientiane, which until it was sacked by the Siamese in 1826, being almost totally destroyed, was known when it superseded Luang Prabang as the capital in 1566, as "the most magnificent city in south-east Asia".

We found that Lao aviation flew directly from Chiangmai to Vientiane, in an hour, but only on a Thursday or a Sunday, however the three-day option proved ideal once Na managed to obtain tickets from our local travel agents. The owner declared that in her long experience she had never been asked for air tickets to Laos. "Tell your friend to take you to Singapore or Penang", she declared defiantly, not only because it would be better business. He held his ground, however, and we eventually boarded the small Lao plane – a 'proper' one since it has them – that was only about a quarter full despite such infrequent departures.

I had seen "Le Parasol Blanc" advertised with 53 bedrooms a restaurant and swimming pool, yet costing only $30 for a double room with satellite television. It was a short distance from the airport down past the Patousai arch standing central in an almost deserted square, but very similar otherwise to the "Arc de

Triomphe". Laos was a French colony from about 1895 until 1954, known as French Indo-China.

There we had an auspicious start when the lady receptionist with a cage of white doves on her left, and an aviary of love-birds on her right, asked "One bed or two, sir?" Emboldened by the friendly scene, I replied, "It is our tenth anniversary". "Oh, how lucky you are", she responded, smiling, "especially with one of those fickle Thais".

That overcome, we settled into our comfortable chalet, and later enjoyed our first meal in a smart restaurant that had a large tree, just like the 'world ash' in act one of Wagner's "Die Walkure", growing in the centre, with orchids clasping its massive bulk. A dark shade-netting was spread overhead from which hung scented flowering creepers. The cuisine was mostly French, a sign of the colony's past and included wild boar, venison and jugged hare, all beautifully prepared,yet costing only about two pounds for the main course.

Na was in his element, too, since they also had a good choice of Thai food, he not being a very adventurous eater, and the staff mostly spoke Thai with a northern accent, so he could chat to them freely. It had proved impossible to buy American dollars, the preferred currency, so I arranged to pay by credit card, but on finding there is also a Lao kip, we decided to change twenty pounds into it as a float. In exchange we were given about 90,000 paper kip - no plural, I imagine - and there was no sign of Lady Bracknell's handbag in which to put them.

When Na went off later to explore, I warned him to beware of right-hand traffic, which he had never seen; the village lad also wanted to see if the Laotians looked different. After an hour, or so, he came back with several T-shirts, and a pack of Lao beer, to show in our village among other small trophies. There he was, chatting to the staff, sitting on a wall, who apparently thought he was a new member of the staff. "Where's Pa-pa"? they had inquired. "Oh, he's watching tennis on television, as usual ".

He had found meanwhile a pleasant man with a motorised samlor known as a 'jumbo', and sensibly arranged for him to pick us up next morning for a four-hour tour of the area. He took us firstly to the central "Pra That Luang" rectangular temple complex with the tallest golden stupa in Laos, and the country's chief symbol of Buddhism as practised by 60% of the population; no other religion is tolerated there by the communist PDR government. "Buddhism has played a vital role in the cultural development of Lao PDR and has greatly influenced the thoughts and behaviour of a large percentage of the population", states a government publication.

We then visited Wat Sisaket, built in 1818 and the only temple to escape the city's destruction ten years later. More than 10,000 Buddhist artefacts are there carefully preserved. In addition very many 15th and 16th Buddhist manuscripts, many on palm leaves, are now being researched and collated throughout the country. But against that, Laos only has one university, Dongdok, established in 1990 from a teachers' college, where students study in uniforms and have very limited basic facilities.

Later our guide took us some miles out to a garden crowded with stone Buddhist groups of every imaginable type. He told us they were much revered, and very old – later I read the garden dated in fact from the mid-thirties, but perhaps that is 'very old' to a young Laotian. We ended our trip by lunching on the bank of the Mekong river, wide and majestic at that point.

Two years' later the plane flew instead from Chiangmai direct to Luang Prabang, so it seemed an ideal opportunity to renew my visa in the beautiful ancient capital, recently declared a "world heritage site" in view of its historical importance until demoted in 1566 – it now has a population of only 16,000 people.

The Lao plane, again nearly empty, flew low giving us fine views of the mountainous terrain with primary monsoon forests, where leopard-cats, rare gibbons and black bears still forage undisturbed. On a plain, east of Luang Prabang, however, archaeologists have found hundreds of stone jars, some more than three metres tall, believed to be about 2,000 years old, and speculate about their purpose. The latest theory is that they were used as sarcophagi for the initial interment of important citizens who were subsequently buried

213

in the ground nearby. A distinctive figure inscribed on many, known as the 'frogman', appears to link them to cultures as far away as Yunnan, and Indonesia.

It was a magnificent sight as the plane swung down suddenly in brilliant sunshine over the twisting Mekong river, its shallows twinkling like jewels, and occasional glimpses of golden temples set on high – the higher the more venerated.

The plane then landed directly at its hanger, ready for bed, and after visa formalities we were taken to our hotel "The Hill of Kites" – the paper variety, since the Laotians delight in kite-flying as do the Thais. The smart receptionist matched the lady at "Le Parasol Blanc". "I have a booking for Mr. and Mrs. Bourke", he said in greeting. "Give it to me to alter, please", I responded. "Why bother?" he replied knowingly. So Na remained unnamed and might even have been one of the PDR's most dreaded terrorists.

We enjoyed the town's only swimming pool and dined almost alone. Next day we visited some superb temples by the river their roofs made in many superimposed tiers, sweeping down almost to the ground in northern style. Many young monks were in evidence, too, their saffron robes and serene demeanour and walk, adding to the tranquil scene; there was almost no traffic, except motorbikes and samlors.

The Royal Palace commissioned by French colonists in 1904, the previous one being in disrepair, combines 'beaux arts', including murals by famous French designers, and traditional Lao artefacts. It was built for King Sisavangvong, and he reigned there until his death in 1959. His vast collection of Buddhist images was on display in cabinets, near gifts from other monarchs. His private chapel contains also an important 1st century Buddha statue from Ceylon. From more modern times there stands his cabinet horn gramophone with a favourite record waiting to be played.

His son the crown prince Watthana, added two more elaborate throne rooms and a wall covered with brilliant Japanese glass mosaics, but all in vain since he was never crowned, and abdicated when the PDR was founded, becoming 'supreme advisor to the President.' So ended a long dynasty dating from the first Lao king who was born near Angkor Wat in Cambodia, and brought Buddhism to Laos in Ad. 1359. Ultimately King Watthana and his family were allowed to die of starvation in caves near the Vietnamese border.

Before leaving the palace, so carefully maintained, I had the worst fall of my life down four white marble steps with no balustrade and water flowing casually across the top one. I was astonished to find all the component parts of my right-hand side intact. Next day however, I was too bruised to undertake a long journey up the Mekong river by longtail boat.

Perhaps it was as well, since on our return to Thailand, I read a fierce tirade against the country by Republican congressman Mark Green of Wisconsin, who has many former Lao Hmong exiles in his constituency, saying it was time for Laos to accept visits from authorised journalists – I had put 'retired journalist' on my visa application, but perhaps my writing was too bad – and mend their attitude to human rights. It concluded that no Americans should travel near Luang Prabang in particular, where he alleged bandits lay in wait. Indeed I felt we had unknowingly supped with the devil.

Now I bid farewell and add some final religious thoughts as only seems appropriate. On my last return to Ireland, I went to a service at Abington church from which little Lucy was buried, and much to my surprise found myself conducting matins for the first time.

Our vicar, who has to oscillate between four or five tiny parishes, failed to turn up for our congregation of only ten people. After a while our oldest parishioner, Joan Bawtree, who saved the church from closure a few years ago, pleading with the bishop to allow its retention some more years while her husband was lay-reader, asked me to deputise. I agreed, sudden as was the request and duly found a prayer for the government about to hold elections, and another for our lady president in her new appointment, but I had no time to find one for my Thai - 'the distant beloved'.

It was when leading the Apostles' Creed that I realised I was in fact affirming my dual religions these past few years, Protestant in Ireland and Buddhist in Thailand, especially where it ends with belief in "the resurrection of the body and the life everlasting. Amen", clearly applicable to both. Buddhist philosophy, furthermore, is based on three prime tenets "tolerance, charity and loving kindness", who could ask for more?

I have long stated in my will that I wish to be cremated where I die since I see no purpose whatsoever in moving people around once they are dead. I will rejoin my George when cremated and hope to die in Thailand where I have been so very happy and the ritual of death is so positive. It is customary for the celebrations to continue for up to five days before the deceased is 'put to the fire', as Na calls it. Everyone who has ever heard of you comes to pay tribute and wish you a serene new life. The mourners wear black or white, and pray and chat while taking rice soup and other refreshments. Sometimes they also play cards discreetly well into the night.

Around the raised bier holding a very brightly coloured catafalque with Buddhist emblems and a photograph, sit three young monks. Among these may well be some who have waved so cheerfully when passing this old foreigner reading on the veranda. Who better to keep me company on my last night, so similar to the little boys in Mozart's "The Magic Flute", "three gentle spirits shall protect you and in the path of truth direct you".

Funeral rhythmic music, like my father heard often on distant tom-toms in Africa, is played for a full day, and on the last morning one is placed on a trolley bearing also many special paper funeral flowers, before it is drawn by friends to the open air funeral pyre near our beautiful village temple. Prayers are recited by the chief monk and sometimes lateral fireworks are released before the cremation that normally takes place at two o'clock. All present wish you well in accordance with the manner in which you have lived this particular life on earth.

Then George will say: "Well Gerard, how WAS Thailand"?
Au Revoir.

ISBN 141200969-3